Victor A Cuadra

The Pocket Essential

STOCK MARKET ESSENTIALS

www.pocketessentials.com

First published in Great Britain 2002 by Pocket Essentials, 18 Coleswood Road, Harpenden, Herts, AL5 1EQ

Distributed in the USA by Trafalgar Square Publishing, PO Box 257, Howe Hill Road, North Pomfret, Vermont 05053

Series Editor: Paul Duncan

A CIP catalogue record for this book is available from the British Library.

ISBN 1-903047-33-1

2 4 6 8 10 9 7 5 3 1

Book typeset by Pdunk
Printed and bound by Cox & Wyman

for Flora, the love of my life...

Acknowledgements

Thanks to... Paul Duncan for giving me the opportunity to write this book. My mom, dad and sister for all the support through the easy and rough times. Mike, Chris and especially the Cruz brothers for providing an amazing work environment and for giving me the opportunity to learn all that I am now sharing through this book.

CONTENTS

1. Introduction

The very first truth you need to know about the stock market is that there are no truths in the stock market, other than: if you sell at a higher price than you bought, you will have a very good chance of making a profit.

Regardless of what all the experts, books and articles say about any aspect of the investment world, the truth is that it is all just opinions, interpretations of events and theories that try to approximate the reality that is the stock market. This, of course, applies to this book as well.

This book is a guided tour through beginner and intermediate concepts, opinions, interpretations and theories about the stock market. Hopefully, it will give you the background information you need to form your own opinions, interpretations and theories about how it works.

The first myth that needs to be dispelled is the financial holy grail. The myth about a system, strategy or plan that is nearly infallible and gives a foolproof chance of making it in the stock market. Having been involved with the stock market for a number of years, and having worked with many of the top traders, I can say with confidence that there is no such thing as the financial holy grail. There are, though, consistent methodologies that can greatly improve the possibilities of profiting in the stock market in the short, intermediate and long term.

All investments, in the stock market or otherwise, have risks, rewards and a possibility of success. You can think of these as three arrows that can't all point in your favour at the same time. At best, two of the three will be in your favour.

For example, the lottery offers exceptional returns and very low risk. You are usually investing (risking) 1 dollar or pound and have the potential to win hundreds, thousands or even millions in return. Even though you have great risk/reward ratio your possibility of success is nearly zero.

When trading futures, also called commodities, there are good possibilities you will be successful, and the potential rewards are very impressive thanks to the leverage available in the futures market and the volatility of most commodities, but you also have great risk of loosing all of your investments very quickly if you make mistakes.

Savings accounts and other banking, interest-based saving vehicles like certificate of deposit, money market accounts etc. have virtually no risk and very high probability of success. But they fall short in the rewards category, having a fixed (and low) return potential.

Finally, stocks offer a somewhat balanced risk/reward/possibility of success ratio. Prepared and conscientious investors have very good possibilities of success with very acceptable risk and reward levels. This is one of the main reasons why many have flocked to invest in the stock market.

Often, the words invest and trade are used as though they are interchangeable. However, within the professional money management community they have very different meanings and many implications attached to them. An investor is generally know as an individual who buys companies and grows his money as the companies perform in the long run. Traders, also called speculators, buy and sell stocks, not companies. Traders don't need to study the long-term performance of companies because they are interested in making a profit from short-term fluctuations of price.

It's important to know your objectives when jumping into the stock market world, and to align them with either the trading or investing philosophies. Being unclear about this will probably result in mixed results in your profit/loss statements as well.

Having a broad picture of the market is very important when analysing individual stocks. The overall market can serve as the background over which you study the company performance and/or its stock price fluctuations. For example, if a stock suddenly drops but the overall market is in the midst of a rally, instead of staying away from this stock it might be a great buying opportunity.

Similar analysis can be done with the industry group or groups where the stock belongs. This approach allows investors and traders to study how stocks are performing compared to their peers and their industry.

The time to analyse individual stocks comes only after you have a picture of the overall market direction. Choosing stocks can be a very laborious task because there are thousands of stocks worldwide. There is no simple way of choosing the right stocks, but the battle-tested approach of dividing and conquering is as good a method as any other. One of the most popular ways of classifying stocks is by their Market Capitalisation value. Stocks are usually classified as small, med (medium) and large cap and each one of these groups has very distinct behaviours associated with them. Large cap stocks are the mega-companies that are market leaders and very reliable. These stocks are usually very stable, and very few events can move their prices significantly, yet they are great anchors against violent market moves and they can produce steady profits over time.

On the other hand, small cap stocks are from small and intermediate companies that might not be as stable as larger companies but they have great potential for growth. Both internal events and events in the market place usually make these stocks move significantly. These stocks are commonly used when looking for aggressive growth or capital gains.

Finally, med cap stocks are somewhere in the middle and they offer a balance between the stability of the large cap stocks and the potential for growth of the small cap stocks. Med cap stocks are rapidly gaining favour amongst traders and investors worldwide.

When it comes to studying the stocks themselves, there are two main schools of thought: Fundamental Financial Analysis and Stock Price Analysis.

Fundamental Financial Analysis is studying the financial performance of the stock by comparing it to its peers in its industry and to other companies and corporations of similar size and make-up.

Stock Price Analysis is studying the price movement of the stock to find prices at which stock prices tend to change direction, and when the stock price falls into prolonged trends.

Regardless of the method used to study stocks, the ultimate objective is to find the fair value of the stock and see the relation between this fair value and the current stock price. Then when this fair value changes for whatever reason, the stock price either rallies or falls to where the new fair value is producing bullish or bearish trends.

It is also extremely important to diversify your portfolio of stocks. Investing or trading stocks from different markets, international or domestic, can do this. Look to have a mix of stocks from at least two of the three market capitalisation groups, and look to have stocks from different industry groups as well. The idea of diversification is to have a basket of stocks that are not all directly or inversely correlated, so that they produce consistent results all the time. Different markets and industries alternate between periods of growth, stagnation and decline, so diversifying your portfolio with stocks from different groups helps to avoid periods where all your portfolio is stagnating or declining.

Whatever methods or ideas you choose to trade and invest make sure you are consistent.

In the last few decades business management has seen many breakthroughs in process control and improvement. What all of these management theories have in common is that all business processes need to be standardised, documented and measured. This allows you to evaluate the efficiency and effectiveness of the business and monitor the performance of the process into the future, so that potential problems can be detected early and major negative consequences avoided.

Trading is no different to any other business discipline. Before you start trading, you should seriously consider standardising, documenting and measuring the process used to choose, buy and sell your stocks. By doing this, you will have the opportunity to find when and where the performance of your strategies starts to deteriorate. Then you will have the opportunity to fine tune it and solve any potential problems.

Finally, stock options and mutual funds are two very different ways of participating in the stock market.

Stock options give you great leverage but add time and many other complexities to trading. Many traders and investors are intimidated by this and do not use options.

Mutual funds are an instant way of diversifying your portfolio with little effort. When investing in mutual funds you are trusting your investment capital to the hands of a professional money manager whose job is to put together a portfolio of stocks following his own methodology. Mutual funds are normally diversified to an extreme, which improves the possibility of success, reduces the risk and the potential returns. Many traders shy away from mutual funds because of their lack of volatility (and therefore lack of large profits).

Note: I have used a variety of terms in this book which may or may not be known to you. For the bewildered, I have included a Glossary at the back of the book.

2. A Short History Of The Stock Market

Stocks were first traded in the middle of the 18th century, but there are records of trading activity dating as far back as the 11th century.

The early precursor to modern stock trading activity first took place, and proliferated, in Western Europe. One of the first known trading exchanges is the Paris Bourse in France during the 12th century. Other ancestors of modern exchanges are the Amsterdam Bourse in the Netherlands, the Deutsche Stock Exchange in Frankfurt and the London Stock Exchange, all of which became active trading centres shortly after the Paris Bourse.

Other European exchanges opened in the 17th and 18th centuries, including those in Belgium, Spain, Portugal and Sweden. When those early exchanges started, stocks were extremely uncommon, so the exchanges first specialised in commodities and currencies.

The first exchange to formally begin trading stocks was Amsterdam's Bourse in 1785. Many other investors around the world rapidly caught wind of the possibilities of the exchange and trade of stocks, and by the mid-19th century many countries outside of Europe were trading securities including the United States, Canada and Australia.

Meanwhile, in the late 18th century, a group of brokers in Philadelphia and New York City began to meet in parks and coffee houses to buy and sell securities. These meetings looked like open auctions, where traders called out names of companies and numbers of shares available looking for the highest bidders. With the end of the American Revolution at the end of the 18th century, the number of securities made available increased dramatically and brokers started to organise themselves so that they could handle the increased volume. In 1800, the Philadelphia Board of Brokers drew up regulations and a constitution, and set up central offices where trading could take place. This organisation was eventually named the Philadelphia Stock Exchange, which is the oldest exchange in the United States. A few years later, in 1817, the New York Stock Exchange was formed.

As the United States and Europe grew and prospered during the 19th century, dozens of exchanges were formed, some of which are still in existence while others were short-lived. For example, the California gold rush of 1849 gave birth to a number of small exchanges where the public could buy shares of mining companies from the area. However, as the gold rush subsided, these California companies moved or went out of existence, causing this California exchanges to go out of business as well.

During the second half of the 19th century, New York City emerged as the primary financial centre of the United States. Within New York, the NYSE (New York Stock Exchange) became one of the most prosperous exchanges in the world, where most of the largest corporations made their shares available to traders and investors. Meanwhile, stocks of smaller companies were still traded by brokers on the streets. In 1908 a group of such brokers formed an organisation called the New York Curb Agency, which later became known as the American Stock Exchange or ASE in 1953.

During the late 19th and early 20th centuries the stock exchanges were very different from what they are today. Those early exchanges were more like a club, where men chatted and spent most of the day socialising. This would be interspersed with short periods of stock-related activities such as trading, or receiving information coming from other parts of the world about developments with corporations, countries or even wars.

In the early 1900s, for the first time, millions of individuals began to purchase stocks. Many new investors entered the stock markets with borrowed money. Stock prices rose steadily as inflated market demands outpaced the increase in the capital value of businesses. Eventually, the imbalance between stock prices and the money behind stocks and companies was unbearable and many decided to pull out of their investments, giving birth to the crash of 1929 in the United States. Prices tumbled so drastically on the NYSE and other exchanges that millions of investors lost all of their savings. Many found themselves in debt and unable to cover their financial responsibilities.

During the years after the crash, most investors refused to look at the stock market as an investment vehicle and, without much flow of new capital, many businesses failed and others reduced their operations significantly. This situation was one of the main causes of the Great Depression of the United States during the 1930s.

The next fifteen years were grim for stocks and companies but the US economy showed sustained strength after World War Two. To prevent stock price manipulation from larger brokers and companies, and to protect smaller investors, the government created the first regulatory agencies. The overall environment became much friendlier to all involved, and with all the technological advances, especially in the area of communications, the stock market once again became a popular place to look for investment profits.

From the 1950s to the 1970s, the exchanges and the stock market grew steadily with few hitches. But by the mid-70s, exchanges became very powerful and stopped serving their original purpose: to create an environment that facilitated trading. Exchanges started to limit direct access to the floor, only allowing members that paid high commissions to directly participate in the exchange activities, thus forcing all other individuals and institutions interested in trading to become clients of the members of the exchange. At this point a small elite of power brokers from within the exchanges controlled the stock market.

The regulatory government agencies in the United States stepped in once more and passed laws that promoted fair play amongst exchanges and traders. One such regulatory law was the Consolidated Tape System, which provided information to investors from all exchanges. The National Market System required that all prices of trading instruments be available simultaneously at each exchange. In response to these and other provisions, many discount brokerage firms opened and trading has now become accessible to the general public as never before.

It is important to note that advances in technology are linked with stock market growth. It started with the telegraph and the telephone, which transmitted relevant information about events that impacted on companies and the economy, and now computers distribute and analyse information. At the moment, personal computers and modern telecommunications allow individuals to see the trade activity from any exchange in the world within seconds, and to respond by placing trades that are intelligently routed back to these exchanges. This effectively allows anyone to participate in any market from the comfort of their home or office.

Computer networks have also allowed exchanges and traders around the world to connect to each other, both within countries and internationally. There are even purely electronic exchanges, like the NASDAQ, where all the trading activities are carried out within a computer network with minimal human intervention. This significantly increases the speed, accuracy and flexibility of all trading activity. Consequently, technology has greatly helped to diminish the obstacles individuals and organisations face when participating in stock trading activities around the world.

In recent years electronic exchanges and globalisation of the world economy have produced a fertile ground for the growth of an open, global securities market. It's an amazing time to follow the events and participate in the financial world.

3. Trading Versus Investing

Many people use the terms trading and investing as if they are interchangeable. However, there are very important differences between a trader and an investor, and it is crucial for anyone's financial well-being in the stock world to clearly declare himself or herself as a trader or an investor.

The simplest way to differentiate traders from investors is by their ultimate goal. Traders use the stock market as a workplace, where they generate part or all of their income by speculating about short-term moves of stocks. Investors place their savings or excess capital in companies they believe in, betting in the longer-term growth of the company.

From this simple distinction, a number of differences can be derived between traders and investors…

- Traders buy and sell stock shares; Investors place their capital behind companies and corporations.

- Traders will have their capital in a particular stock for a short period of time. The time a trader has their money in the market can vary from minutes to days and sometimes weeks but rarely will they stay invested in a stock for a month or longer. Investors in turn are in for the longer run. They put their money behind a company and will stay in for months or years.

- For a trader, other participants in the market are his foes and he is competing against them and trying to gain every possible advantage over them. For an investor, other participants in the market are his allies, and he is interested in the consensus amongst investors.

- Traders spend a great amount of time studying the markets every day, or at the least every week. Investors do their research more sporadically; every few months or years when they feel it is time to change their portfolio of companies.

It is very easy to see and comprehend the differences between traders and investors once these distinctions have been made. And the reason why it's so important to declare if one is an investor or a trader is to help define your mission and goals when participating in the stock market.

You must be very clear about the purpose and objectives of your business before you consider anything else. The action steps and activities are drastically different depending upon whether you are trading or investing, so your very first task is to understand your motivation, needs and expectations. Then you can declare yourself as a trader or an investor. Once this is done, everything will flow much easily.

4. What Is A Stock Exchange?

An exchange is an organised market in which financial instruments are bought and sold. An exchange can specialise in one type, or it can offer a variety of instruments to its members. These Financial instruments can be, for example, stocks or securities, stock options, bonds, futures or commodities, or futures options.

The main purpose of an exchange is to facilitate the buying and selling of any of these instruments for as many individuals and organisations as possible.

Most stock exchanges have a specific location where commissioned or paid intermediaries, called brokers, conduct all the buying and selling activities. But with the advances in technology, electronic exchanges commonly called ECNs are becoming more and more popular throughout the world. Electronic exchanges like NASDAQ are run by powerful computers which have automated many of the processes commonly performed by brokers or members of the exchange. This generally improves speed and reliability, and brings buyers and sellers closer together. Electronic exchanges have restored to market participants the feeling of buying or selling directly without intermediaries.

The major exchanges in the United States include the New York Stock Exchange (NYSE), the NASDAQ and the American Stock Exchange (AMEX). All three are located in New York - a fact that is becoming less and less relevant with advances in technology. In the United States there are nine smaller regional stock exchanges that operate in Boston, Philadelphia, Massachusetts, Cincinnati, Chicago, Los Angeles, California, Miami, Salt Lake City, San Francisco and Spokane.

Worldwide there are major exchanges in most industrialised countries. Amongst the world's largest are the London Stock Exchange (LSE) in the United Kingdom, the Deutsche Bourse in Germany, the Paris Bourse in France, the Toronto Stock Exchange (TSE) in Canada and the Hong Kong Stock Exchange in China.

Stock exchanges serve crucial roles in national and global economies. They encourage investment by providing an organised market place for buyers and sellers to trade stocks and other financial instruments.

Many companies like the stock exchanges because they can issue stocks and bonds to obtain capital, and hence grow and expand their businesses. Companies make stock available in what is called the primary market, commonly under guidance and help of investment bankers. Companies then receive the proceeds of stock sales in the primary market, leaving them with capital to grow their business. After this is done, they are not involved in the trading of their stock.

This stock made available by the companies is then offered in the secondary market through a stock exchange, where investors and traders get the opportunity to participate by buying and selling company shares and possibilities of profit or losses are realised for outsiders of the company.

Stock exchanges have a number of rules and regulations to protect investors, and to ensure that buyers are treated fairly without risk of unfair price manipulation of the markets.

Market Makers

Traditional exchanges usually have members, which sometimes are called market makers. Market makers are major firms, usually brokerage houses, that act as competitors in a particular exchange. In the United States, NASDAQ is the main exchange that has exposed the market maker information to the general public, and NASDAQ has approximately 500 firms that act as such entities.

Market makers are major firms that are members of the exchange and through which all transactions in the exchange are channelled. Any individual or institution that wants or needs to buy or sell stock in NASDAQ needs to place their order through a market maker.

The way these exchanges work is by allowing competition between market makers for customer orders. Each market maker is allowed to display buy and sell quotations for any given stock. When a customer is interested in buying or selling shares, an order is placed in the exchange and it is filled with the best offer amongst the market makers.

Some market makers hold large quantities of stock, and they allow their customers to buy and sell these shares from their inventory at increasing speed (and sometimes offering other advantages to their customers), thus keeping the transaction away from competing market makers.

Thanks to computer automation, there are screens that show the entire list of bids (buy quotations) and offers (sell quotations) for a stock that include the name of the market maker, the number and price of shares offered. This screen is called a Level II screen.

Specialists

In exchanges where there has not been a complete automation of procedures, like in the NYSE, there are individuals that work in the trading floor of the exchange called market specialists.

The trading floor of an exchange is a room where brokers meet and perform all their transactions during trading sessions. The floor of the NYSE, for example, is a huge room of about 1700 square meters where brokers and floor traders conduct their daily business.

Market specialists manage all the transactions related to a particular stock in a designated area of the floor of the exchange. They are specialised brokers that deal only with a handful, and sometimes only one, stock. They are part of the exchange, and their function is to act as dealers to match bids and offers of different floor traders, and to overlook the trading activity in an attempt to balance supply and demand of the stocks they work with.

In the NYSE, market makers handle all orders above 1200 shares. All transactions under 1200 shares are routed to specialised brokers via computers. Each exchange with market specialists have rules so that trading is standardised.

ECNs

An ECN is a special type of market maker, which is completely computerised. Individual traders, institutions or even other market makers can use an ECN to place orders in the exchange through completely computerised systems.

ECNs are usually branches of major brokerage houses that offer their services to any individual or organisation that wants to place orders directly to the exchange without intermediaries. Traders that place orders directly to the exchange through ECNs are said to have 'direct access trading.' And it's usually reserved for day traders that need great speed and reliability to have the ability to buy and sell shares of any stock within minutes or even seconds. One of the most commonly known ECNs is ISLAND, which is owned and operated by Datek Online Trading.

ECNs maintain their own 'book' of orders. This means that ECNs have a list of their customers who are buying and selling a particular stock, with the number of shares and the price they are willing to pay. The ECNs with a greater number of clients and with a bigger volume of shares traded per stock can often offer their clients the option to trade stocks within the ECN. So a trader might buy shares from another ECN customer without ever interacting with the exchange, increasing the speed of the transaction and often allowing the ECN to give better rates on commissions to both the buyer and the seller.

Order Flow

Unbeknownst to many, their orders change hands many times before they ever reach the stock exchange. Each individual trader or investor should research the order flow to ensure that it is not harming their performance in the trading or investing game.

For investors, order flow rarely comes into play as they are into long-term commitments with the stocks they purchase. This means the speed and accuracy of the execution of their buying and selling orders are not paramount to their strategies.

On the other hand, traders who need to buy and sell stocks within minutes or hours need the fastest, most efficient and accurate execution of their orders. Since they are trying to profit from much smaller price moves, unnecessary delays in order execution can turn their winning trades into losers.

It is obvious that the exchanges that are fully computerised and have all procedures fully automated are greatly favoured by day traders. After all, the main purpose of computers is to allow for the processing of many tasks at speeds that are not available otherwise. The speed and accuracy that computers provide means that exchanges can offer a wealth of information previously unavailable because it was impossible to compile and distribute it in the past.

Electronic exchanges like NASDAQ are the ideal battleground for traders that specialise in fast, short-term trades that last a few minutes. Longer-term traders and investors don't gain a significant advantage and it is probably best for them to use all the available exchanges.

When a trader places an order to buy, for example, AABC stock in the NASDAQ exchange, he will place an order through his broker. If the broker is an ECN, it will place the order directly on the exchange and the order will be filled according to the supply and demand of the AABC stock at that moment.

It is possible that his broker is not an ECN, in which case the broker would have to receive his order, and then relay it to the Exchange through an ECN or a market maker. This will obviously take more time, because there is an additional intermediary between the trader and the exchange.

When the order is received by the exchange, it is placed in an electronic 'book' of orders, and your order is filled accordingly to supply and demand rules of the exchange. Normally, the buy orders at higher prices and the sell orders at lower prices are filled first.

Once the order to buy shares is filled, a confirmation message is relayed back to the broker. The confirmation number returns to the trader the same way the order reached the exchange. Many times traders need to know the details of the fill of their order as soon as possible because their trades might last a few hours or even minutes. The time of execution of the entire round trip is paramount for traders.

A second scenario is an investor looking to buy, for example, stock XYZ from a traditional exchange, like the NYSE. In this case, the investor places an order to buy 100 shares of stock XYZ through his broker. The only option to trade in the NYSE exchange is to go through a market maker. The broker relays the order to a market maker, who has his floor trader in the exchange place the order with the specialist. The floor specialist fills the order according to the rules of the NYSE and gives the floor trader the details of the fill of the order.

The floor trader informs the market maker of the results, and the market maker informs the investor. As you might imagine, the information of the resulting trade takes much longer than when working with fully automated exchanges, but for the majority of investors a few minutes is not a great concern because they are normally looking to hold to their positions for long periods of time.

In some instances, brokers sell the trader or investor's orders at wholesale prices to a 'bigger broker' who then places the order with the market maker. This is how some of the discount brokerages firms are capable of offering their clients very low commissions for their trades. But the time it takes the order to be filled and have a confirmation back is considerably greater. This is unacceptable for most traders.

Bid And Ask Prices

There is a market because in every exchange there are buyers and sellers for every stock. The bid and the ask of a particular stock is the best price offered amongst the buyers and the best price offered amongst the sellers respectively.

When an investor places an order to buy 100 shares of a stock, his order is matched with the best ask price in the market. Inversely, if a trader places an order to sell 100 shares of a stock his order will be matched with the best possible ask.

For most stocks, there are dozens and sometimes hundreds or thousands of interested buyers and sellers at any given moment. But not all of them are willing to take just any price available in the market. Normally these market participants give their brokers special types of orders called stop and limit orders. Stop and limit orders are buy and sell instructions that depend upon the price of the stock. These stop and limit orders eventually become the bid and ask prices. Stop and limit orders are explained later in this book, so don't worry if you are not completely familiar with these terms.

Electronic exchanges can now make available to the public real-time lists of buyers and sellers with their bid and ask prices. This allows traders to see who is buying and selling, how much they want and at what price. This gives traders a greater depth of understanding of what the market is doing at any given time. This data is called 'Level II data' and is not yet available in all exchanges. NASDAQ was the first exchange to fully and freely distribute this data to the public.

5. Analysing The Market

The market is a term that has been used by many people in many different ways. For the purpose of this book, the market is a collection of stocks belonging to different industry groups related by one or more common characteristics.

This definition still allows for very different types of markets. For example, all stocks belonging to any active industry groups in the United States compose the US Market. Stocks that participate in a particular exchange usually tend to have certain common characteristics. For example, the NASDAQ exchange can also be called a market composed mainly of technology oriented and new economy stocks. The European Telecommunications Market is made by all stocks that belong to different sectors in the telecommunications market in Europe etc.

So when talking about the market, it is necessary to specify which market. Not qualifying the specific market implies a reference to the overall market, and it is still not clear if it is a reference to the world market, or the market of a particular nation or region.

At any one time, a market will have stocks that are in trending, consolidation or sideways moves, or declining. Still, it's always possible to find the overall market sentiment. The most common and straightforward method used to determine the market sentiment is by studying different market indices.

Major Market Indices

A market index is a formula that uses the prices of a group of stocks that belong to a market to calculate the sentiment of a sector or the overall market.

One of the best-known market indices is the Dow Industrial Average in the United States. It is so popular that it is simply called the market by many, and when they say "the market was up 50 points today" they are referring to the Dow Industrial Average being up fifty points from yesterday's closing number. The Dow Industrial Average is a mathematical formula that uses the prices of 30 major industrial US stocks. This index was created with the intention of reflecting the overall direction of stock prices of the different industrial sectors of the United States.

More recently, the NASDAQ 100 index has increased in popularity in the United States. The NASDAQ 100 index is a cross-section of what is being called new economy stocks. This index is composed mostly of technology and Internet stocks that have had outstanding performance in the last few years. New economy stocks, especially technology stocks, have given investors and traders great results in the last few years. This success has been so extraordinary that the NASDAQ 100 index has quickly caught up with the Dow Industrial Average in popularity as a tool to gauge the market sentiment. Keep in mind that the Dow Industrial Average has been in existence for more than 100 years, while the NASDAQ 100 is only a dozen years old.

Similar to any stock, market indices have an opening price, a high, a low and a closing price for every trading session. Many people study the price movement of these indices in an attempt to find the overall direction of the market. This can be a very powerful tool as it can show an overall bias on the direction of the stocks that compose the market.

The overall sentiment of the market is commonly used as a background when studying individual stock movement. So, if the overall sentiment of the market is positive, it can be assumed that most stocks will tend to rise with the market, so sudden drops in prices can be considered as buying opportunities. This assumption is based on the fact that most stock prices follow their peers, and consequently their major market index. The catch is that you have to find the appropriate market index for the stocks you are trading.

The most popular indices in the British stock market, and more specifically the London Stock Market, are published by FTSE International (you can find detailed information about FTSE at www.ftse.com) which formulates and calculates, in real time, the values of a number of indices. In the United Kingdom the FTSE 100 is the equivalent of the Dow Industrial Average in the United States. The FTSE 100 is an index composed of the top 100 companies in the United Kingdom based on market capitalisation - market capitalisation is explained later in this book so don't worry if you are not familiar with the term yet.

For the German Bourse, the DAX is the major index considered as the market. The DAX is an index maintained and published by the German Bourse, and like the others described earlier, it's a cross-section of the major companies in the German Stock Exchange.

All indices don't necessarily represent entire markets from a particular country. There are many indices published by exchanges, financial institutions and other organisations that are meant to offer guidance about the sentiment of specific areas of the major markets. The most common segments that are targeted by these indices are industry-specific groups of stocks.

Industry Groups

Any nationwide market, like the United States, United Kingdom, Germany etc., has stocks from companies and corporations that can be grouped by the industry they are in. This is particularly useful for individuals and organisations that specialise in the research, investment and trade of stocks of a particular industry group.

The interaction and performance of every company in an industry has a major effect on individual stock. Entire industry groups usually move in synchronicity. They are usually directly correlated, but some subgroups can be inversely correlated to the movement of the overall industry.

Since the stocks of a particular industry group are linked, when an index is calculated for that specific group then all the advantages described in the above section apply for this industry group. It then is possible to find the overall market direction of the industry group and use it as a guideline when studying individual stocks.

Segregating stocks into industry groups is extremely useful for individuals and organisations that focus their research, and develop their expertise and market awareness in a specific industry. For example, an individual who is a software engineer by trade can specialise in trading or investing in technology stocks, particularly in stocks of software development companies because he has industry expertise. He might know or be able to easily and accurately identify market leaders and emerging technologies in software development that could become successful business enterprises. This individual would focus his efforts on the Software Development Industry group, and would use a Software Development Index to evaluate the overall sentiment of the market to help him in his trading or investing decisions.

Amongst the most commonly followed industry groups are Aerospace And Defense, Airlines, Automobiles, Biotechnology, Business-To-Business, Chemicals, Computer Hardware, Computer Software, Consumer Products, E-Commerce, Energy & Utilities, Engineering & Construction, Financial Services, Food, Gaming, Healthcare, Hotels And Lodging, Insurance Companies, Entertainment, Internet, Media And Entertainment, Mining And Metals, Networking, Oil Services, Paper And Forest, Pharmaceuticals, Railroads, Real Estate, Retail, Semiconductors, Storage, Technology, Telecommunications, Waste Management, Wireless & Mobile Devices etc.

6. Stocks

The Encarta online encyclopaedia (http://encarta.msn.com) defines stocks as certificates representing shares of ownership in a corporation. These certificates entitle the holders to share in the profits of the company, which are paid out at intervals in the form of dividends. Besides claims on company profits, stock-holders are entitled to a share in the sale of the company if it is dissolved. They can also vote in person or by proxy for corporation officers, inspect the accounts of the company at reasonable times, vote at stockholders' meetings and, when the company issues new stock, have priority to buy a certain number of shares before they are offered for public sale.

However, despite these benefits, the main reason individuals and organisations buy and sell stocks from a company is to profit from the changes in valuation of the stock prices. Stock prices of companies that outperform their peers and become market leaders tend to increase in value and, like any other investment stocks, can be an extremely valuable tool in growing your capital and generating income.

Why Own Them?

In the last few years, stocks have strengthened their position as the ideal investment vehicle for the vast majority of individuals and institutions looking to grow their money – to invest. The explosion of technology and the influx of new traders into the markets has increased the volatility of stocks, making stocks very popular amongst the trading community as well.

The economy is fluid and in constant change so there will always be markets in growth mode and expanding, and always markets that slow down and get stagnant. Throughout history, with few exceptions, markets have behaved cyclically. They have leading performance eras then fade into the background to resurface again at a later time. There will always be a need for products and services in the world. There will always be companies that will fill these needs and lead their industry and others that will grow and expand their services.

Bearing this in mind, you can see why the stock world presents itself as a constantly changing realm of possibilities for profits. There is such a diversity in stocks that there will always be a group of stocks that have the potential to match any goals and/or expectations or traders and investors, regardless of whether the market is in growth or recession.

There are many options when searching for stocks as investment vehicles. There are steady mega-companies that are industry leaders, upcoming firms with enormous potential for growth, companies that have had difficulties and have fallen out of favour but are expected to turn around their performance etc. Within these categories, you can specify other qualities that meet your investing or trading needs more precisely.

There are other investment and trading vehicles that might better fit your needs but stocks are the most flexible and adaptable.

In this chapter you will study different types of stocks, and different methods commonly used to analyse them.

Types Of Stocks - Market Capitalisation

Market capitalisation of a stock can be defined as the total value that the market participants give a stock. It is a very simple number calculated using the following formula:

Market Capitalisation = Float x Stock Price

The float is the total number of shares made available by the company. So, if a company offers 100,000 shares to the public, and the value of the shares are $75, then the market capitalisation is $7,500,000. This is a relatively small number - large companies reach billions of dollars in market capitalisation.

Why is it important to study the market capitalisation? To help find stocks that match a certain profile needed to meet particular investor needs.

Companies are usually divided in large cap, mid cap and small cap, where cap means capitalisation, as in market capitalisation. Even though there are many different numbers used as limits to place companies in one of these groups, there are standard behavioural characteristics tied to each group.

A few years ago, a small cap company was defined as one with a valuation of less than $250 million. More recently, it was generally agreed that $500 million marked the ceiling on small companies. Some now define small cap stocks as companies with market capitalisation up to $1 billion and mid cap stocks from $1 billion to $5 billion. Large cap, then, is $5 billion and above; some say $10 billion and above. And others have added giant cap to represent companies that investors have valued at more than $100 billion.

Still, the consensus is that stock prices of small capitalisation companies have a much greater opportunity to move and to produce significant returns to investment in a relatively short period of time. But, as always, with the greater return potential comes greater risk. The volatility of the stock price can lead the stock to either significantly positive or significantly negative moves.

Large capitalisation stocks are usually the big names in major industries. These are very stable companies. They are usually diversified and so big that it is difficult to find news that will shake their foundation and significantly change their stock price. Thus, these stocks are normally considered less risky but also provide more modest returns.

Finally, mid cap stocks are somewhere in between and are rapidly increasing in popularity amongst traders and investors because they have very respectable growth potential with less risk than small cap stocks.

Market capitalisation is a major factor when building any stock portfolio. Ideally, a portfolio will be diversified to include different types of stocks, and one of the most valuable characters used to distinguish two stocks as significantly different is their market capitalisation. Diversification is discussed later in this book.

Evaluating Stocks

When the type of stock to be included in a portfolio has been decided, you must evaluate different stocks to help decide which you want to invest or trade in.

When evaluating stocks you must always find out if the stock is under- or overvalued. It is fair to say that this is the ultimate question in the investment game, and everyone asks themselves this question when studying a stock or any investment vehicle.

With stocks, there is a wealth of information available for the study of the financial health of the company on its own and in comparison to its peers, and the valuation of the stock.

Stock prices are always oscillating around their fair value. When a stock separates itself from its fair value to the upside, less and less investors and institutions will be willing to purchase shares. In fact, the market participants will resist paying for the stock at these higher prices. This is commonly called a resistance level.

Conversely, if the stock falls below its fair value the market participants will buy expecting the price to return to fair value or higher. They will support these low prices by buying shares. This is commonly called a support level.

Stock prices are influenced by many different factors. Amongst the most commonly looked at are: the financial health of the company, the health of the industry where the stock belongs, its performance relative to other stocks in its industry and the overall performance.

When one or more of these factors change, the fair value of the stock will change as well, and the stock price will move to adjust to the new fair value. This is what constitutes stock rallies and declines, which are also called trends. If any factor or circumstance changes and the fair value of the stock is perceived to be lower, then the stock will fall and establish a down trend until the price reaches the new fair value. Inversely, if the fair value of the stock increases the prices will rally upward establishing an up trend.

For example, Qualcom, Inc.'s stock fair value was around $40 per share, and its stock moved in a sideways channel between $30 and $50 per share for a few years. During 1999 and 2000 they delivered a new mobile communication technology called CDMA, which was said that was going to be used by 70-90% of the mobile phones in the world in the next 10 years. The stock rose from its trading value to a high of $800 per share in about 1 year because of the dramatic effect the news about the new technology had on the perceived fair value of the company stock. With potential earnings of that size, revenues of the company were sure to skyrocket as well thus the perceived value of the stock went off the charts. We will revisit the Qualcom example later.

So most, if not all, of the techniques commonly used will have the objective of finding the fair value of the stock. So how do you find out how this fair value relates to its current price?

Studying Financial Fundamental Information

Through studying the financial information of a stock it is possible to draw conclusions about the financial health of the institution, and the relative health of the institution in regards to its industry and other similar companies.

Study of financial fundamental information can discern how the company is performing, and ultimately how its stock is valued within its industry or market.

The most commonly used measures are Earnings, Earnings Per Share (EPS) and Price Earnings Ratio (PE Ratio). Here are brief explanations:

Earnings

One of the most basic measures used to evaluate how a company is performing is their earnings. Earnings are the most direct expression of how well the company is performing, i.e. the greater (positive) the earnings, the better the company is performing.

Earnings are the ultimate indication if a company is successful or not, but by itself it offers very little insight on the valuation of the company's stock. A large corporation that has $50 million in earnings might not be as financially successful as a company that has $20 dollars in earnings. A typical example would be a large corporation, which is operating on expenses of $500 million, while the smaller corporation has expenses in the order of $50 million. In other words, the margin of earnings is significantly smaller for the larger corporation. And regardless of how earnings alone are studied, they still offer little insight on how the stock price is related to the company's performance and the valuation of the stock price.

Earnings Per Share (EPS)

When you invest you are not buying and selling whole companies. You are buying and selling stock shares from the company, and it is important to have an idea of how valuable the stock is. Dividing the earnings by the total number of shares available from the company is the most direct way to see how much of the company's earnings each individual stock represents. This shows how valuable a share is.

When companies are publicly traded in a trading exchange, there will be a finite number of shares available for trading. The total number of shares made available for trading is commonly referred to as the float.

So, if a company has 200 million shares in the market and has profits of $100 million, the EPS will be 0.5$/share. A different way of looking at this would be to say that each share represents 0.5$ of the profits of the company.

This number will give instant insight into the value of a share in regard to the company's earnings.

Here is the formula for calculating the EPS:

$$EPS = \frac{Earnings}{Float}$$

Note: when a stock split occurs, the company is doubling the number of shares in their float. When this happens, the value each share represents in regard to the earnings immediately drops to half. Looking at the formula you can see how the earnings are divided by the float, only the float will be a number twice as large.

For example, if a company has a float of 200 million shares and profits of $100 million, the EPS is 0.5$/share. If a 2:1 (two for one) stock split occurs, there will be twice as many shares available for trading, while the earnings numbers remain unchanged. Looking at the formula, this would make the EPS instantly drop to a half of its prior value.

EPS numbers are great tools to find the inherent values of the shares of a company in regard to the financial performance of the company. However, this number offers no help to you when you try to analyse the price of the stock, which is the final goal of any investor.

Price-Earnings Ratio

Given that you need to evaluate a stock to find if it is under- or overvalued, you need to include the current price of the stock in the equation. This is commonly done by studying the price-earnings ratio of a stock.

The formula for the PE Ratio of a stock is as follows:

$$PERatio = \frac{Price of Stock}{EPS}$$

The PE Ratio is a value that shows the relation between the price of the stock and the earnings per share of the company. If you substitute the EPS formula into this equation, you will have:

$$PERatio = \frac{Price of Stock}{Earnings/Stock}$$

This number gives a measure of how the stock of any company is valued based on its earnings, and the inherent value of each share available in the market. So, if you place values in the formula you can start to see how this formula works:

For example, if ABC company has its stock prices at $60, while it has $300 million in profits and 100 million shares in its float, you will have the following formula:

$$PERatio = \frac{60}{300M/100M} = 20$$

Now you have a measure that includes the stock price, earnings and the inherent value of each share. But how do you know if 20 is good or bad? The answer is by comparing the PE Ratio with the average PE Ratio of companies in its same industry, other companies similar in size, and/or its direct competitors.

The objective of this analysis is to compare the PE Ratio of the company to a collection of companies with similar make-up. A great place to start is the index of the industry where the company belongs.

You must find out if the company's PE Ratio is greater or lower than the average. If significantly lower, this would mean that the stock price is probably undervalued, while if significantly higher, this would mean that the stock price is probably overvalued. Still, keep in mind that these are somewhat subjective comparisons, and major differences between the PE Ratio of the company and the average of a group of stocks where it belongs might represent actual financial problems of the company or industry dominance by the subject company or a competitor.

The PE Ratios of companies, sectors and industries can be found in a multitude of resources on the World Wide Web, from brokerage firms or transaction dealers, and different financial services listed in Resource Materials at the end of this book.

Now back to the Qualcom example. When industry experts projected that 70-90% of the mobile devices in the world would be using Qualcom's CDMA technology in the next 10-15 years, the expectations of their potential profits, thus their earnings expectations, multiplied about 100 fold. And in looking at the PE Ratio formula, you will find that if you multiply your earnings by 100, the PE Ratio will fall dramatically, leaving the stock as severely undervalued in comparison with its industry.

There is one important detail that needs to be said about the Qualcom example, and the market in general. Looking carefully at the last paragraph you can see that expected revenues of the company affected the price of the stock significantly. It's commonly said that the market is a forward-looking animal. By this, it is meant that future expected performance is even more important than the most recent financial numbers.

It is as important, if not more, to use the formula with values of future expected EPS numbers when analysing the PE Ratio of a stock. This will give an indication of where the company might be in the future. Financial analysts that cover (or follow) stocks commonly offer future EPS numbers.

Fundamental financial information is normally updated every few months, so this type of information is commonly used by longer term investors as their main source of information to make trading decisions. Some short-term traders use financial fundamental information to find stocks of companies with specific characteristics then perform additional short-term analysis for their trading.

Studying Stock Price Information

Regardless of what method is used to analyse stocks, fundamental financial information or price data, the goal is the same: to find the fair value of the stock so that you can compare this fair value to its current price.

As described earlier, the price movement of any stock oscillates around its fair value, and goes up or down when the circumstances of the stock, the industry or the market change.

The study of price data as the main guide to buying and selling stocks and other investment vehicles is a discipline that has fascinated many individuals and organisations in the last century. It has drawn many professionals from other walks of life to the financial arena like mathematicians, physicists and talented individuals from many other scientific fields. This discipline is commonly referred to as technical analysis.

Technical price analysts of stocks come from the hypothesis that the market as a whole is composed by a great number of individual traders and investors. Each one of these participants will know something, or have some information about the market, and they will use this knowledge to decide their outlook of a particular stock. Every single participant votes by buying or selling shares. Furthermore, not one participant or any subgroup of participants can ever know everything there is to know about a company that can affect the market. Assuming this hypothesis is true, it can be stated that by analysing the final votes (and/or non-votes) of all the participants, it is possible to calculate the most accurate outlook for a stock, and show how the market is behaving in any given moment. The votes of the participants are the buy and sell orders that are placed every day, and these orders are ultimately what makes markets move.

Regardless of who you are, it will never be possible to know absolutely everything about a company, the industry and the market where it trades. But it will always be possible to study how all the participants of a particular market are voting at any time.

Not even company insiders can consistently benefit from their knowledge, since they do not always know what is happening with their competitors and the market. Also, in most countries, investment and trading laws restrict individuals who are privy to sensitive information about any company. Normally an individual can only be an insider of one company at a time, or a very few select companies in special cases.

Stepping back, let's look at how to study price information: To study a stock using only price data, much more than the last price is needed. Detailed records of past prices of the stock are required. Having only the last price to study is similar to giving someone today's temperature for a city he is not familiar with and ask him to choose the clothes he will take for a week stay in a couple of months. Knowing that today it is 20 degrees Celsius at your destination can be very misleading, and he will want to know what the average temperature is, and how much the temperature can change in a short period of time etc. The only way to know this information is by referring to temperature charts of the last months or years. Similarly, studying historical records of stock prices is fundamental to making informed investing decisions about a stock. Current prices alone are not enough!

For any stock there will be thousands or even millions of shares changing hands through many transactions every day. So it's not always practical to study historical price data looking at every transaction. For this reason, the price data is usually condensed and shown for certain time periods. For example, it is very common to see daily information about a stock. This daily information can include the price at which the stock started trading which is commonly referred to as the open, the highest price traded during the day (or the high), the lowest price during the day (or the low) and the last traded price during the day (or the close). Also, the number of shares traded (the volume) and the number of transactions are often given as well.

There are many traders and investors that hold their stock for many different lengths of time. There are traders that just hold their positions for a few minutes, others for a few days, others for weeks, months or even years. Because of this, and thanks to technology, it is also common to see price data for minutes, hours, days, weeks, months and years. Many people work with the open, high, low, close and volume for stock ABC for the first five minutes, and every five minutes thereafter, of a trading day. Or price data representing every month of the year. Their objective always remains the same - to find the fair value of the stock, in order to find how this fair value compares to its current price.

When studying price data to find the fair value, it is essential to first have an idea of approximately how long the position (your stock) is to be held, so that you can choose a time period that serves the trading strategy. If the investment entitles holding the positions for several months, it is very difficult to study the market using five-minute time intervals. If the plan is to day trade it will be very difficult to make sense of what the market does through the life of the trade by looking at weekly, or daily, time periods.

Another very common way to view price data is through price charts. There are many different types of price charts, but the most common type will have vertical bars for each time period (for example, one bar per day) that has a left tick representing the open and a right tick that represents the closing price. Charts are very powerful visual tools that can be used to get a good idea of how the stock prices have behaved in the past.

As mentioned before, the study of price data is commonly called technical analysis. There have been much work done to forward this discipline, and many opinions have been cast, both favourable and unfavourable, about it. Technical analysis uses statistics and mathematics to study price data. By learning about the past and current behaviour of stocks, it can find out if a stock is moving sideways around its fair value, or trending (going up or down). By using the language of mathematics, it is possible to calculate how stocks are behaving by following a consistent methodology. This helps to avoid subjective interpretations.

There is a wide variety of technical analysis tools to evaluate stocks, and there are many of these techniques listed and explained in the References Materials section. To give a flavour of what technical analysis looks like, here are three indicators commonly used to study stocks:

Moving Average

A moving average is an average of the last N number of closing prices, where N is the number of time periods included in the average. If you are working with daily information, adding the closing prices of the last fifty days and dividing the result by 50 will give you a 50 moving average. It's called a moving average because after the close of the next trading day, the oldest day is dropped and the new day is added to calculate the average. So the window of data used to calculate the average moves forward with every time period.

This technique offers a number near the middle of the price range of the last 50 bars (on the chart), which could be thought of as a potential fair value of the price for the last fifty days. Following the idea that stock prices oscillate around their fair value, a possible strategy is to buy when the prices of the stock fall significantly below the 50 bar average, and/or sell when they raise significantly above.

What is significant? This varies with different statistical and mathematical tools. For example, some will say that whenever prices reach two standard deviations below the average, the stock is oversold and a buy signal is raised. But don't limit yourself to this. There is a whole world of statistical and mathematical formulas to describe when the market is under- or overvalued.

2 Moving Averages

By using one average, it is possible to see where the price currently is compared to where it has traded in the recent past. But using one average will not help whenever a stock rallies or falls because its fair value has changed. For this, an option is to explore the use of two moving averages that use different numbers of time periods.

The common usage is to have one of the moving averages include a large number of time periods, and the second a shorter amount of time periods. When these averages have been calculated, the short (or fast) average reacts much faster to price changes and is used to identify market direction. The longer (or slow) average shows the longer-term market direction because it reacts slowly to price changes. If the slow average crosses over or under the fast average, this is normally interpreted as a change in market direction and might be the start of a trend.

Stochastic

The stochastic indicator is commonly used to find out when a stock is under- or overvalued. This indicator takes the highest high and the lowest low of a certain time period, and shows where in this range the most recent price is, where 100 is the highest high and 0 is the lowest low. If the indicator gives a reading close to 50, the stock is considered to be near its fair value.

Financial Analyst Ratings

Eventually, you will understand and begin to use fundamental financial information and price data to analyse stocks. You are not the only person doing this! There are specialists, called financial analysts, whose job is to use all the techniques explained earlier in this book (and other techniques that have not been covered) to produce and publish a short, intermediate and long-term outlook of stocks.

Financial analysts are usually individuals, backed by large financial institutions like brokerage houses that are respected in the industry, who have resources and time available to study individual companies. These analysts have lists of stocks that they follow, and they have a particular opinion of these stocks.

These analysts will give ratings to different stocks ranging from strong sell to strong buy. These ratings are a valuable guide for investors as to the general market sentiment about a particular stock, and about results of the analysts' research, which might have included price data, financial information, industry expertise etc.

The most commonly used ratings are:

- Strong Sell - Stay away from this stock unless you are thinking of short selling it.
- Sell - There are issues in one or more areas for this stock. Do not buy.
- Market Underperform - There are concerns about the performance of the stock. Seriously consider a short sell.
- Neutral - There are no clear bullish or bearish signs. Monitor the stock for future developments.
- Market Perform - This stock is stable but average and will probably give modest returns.

- Market Outperform - The stock is a stable vehicle where to invest your money.
- Buy - Stock has solid current and future performance expectations. Seriously consider buying this stock.
- Strong Buy - Stock is a market star. Buy now!

Not all analysts will have ratings for every stock. As mentioned before, analysts have a list of stocks they are following. The stocks that are in an analyst's list are said to be covered by the analyst, so don't expect every analyst to have a public outlook of all stocks.

Also, it is normal to have more than one analyst cover a stock, so the job is to find the ratings from all the analysts that are covering the subject stock. Look for a consensus or agreement between them for the future direction of the stock.

It is extremely valuable to be aware of the age of the rating. These ratings age very quickly, so this information needs to be used as soon as possible after they are published. Many people follow analyst recommendations, so stocks raise and fall drastically very quickly after they are made public. Analyst ratings serve as a way to change the agreed fair value of a stock, which usually sends many investors and traders into action immediately.

Other Factors

Two very desirable traits of any stock you pick are liquidity and volatility.

In the stock world, liquidity is directly related to how many shares, how many transactions and how many participants are playing the stock on a day-to-day basis. Liquidity can greatly affect the performance of anyone's trading or investing, especially when moving large amounts of shares. If the market has poor liquidity and an individual or institution needs to sell a large quantity of shares, there might not be enough buyers to support all the shares and the price at which these shares will be sold will vary immensely.

For example, assume you are monitoring a stock where there are only 10 buyers looking for 1,000 shares each and their orders are placed as follows: 2 buyers at $15, 4 buyers at $14.75, 3 buyers at $14.50 and 1 buyer at $14.25. Then comes along a trader needing to sell all of his 10,000 shares. This trader will initially see that the bid for this stock is at $15 a share, but when he places his order to sell all 10,000 shares he will go down the list of buyers and will end with prices ranging from $14.25 to $15.

This is a simple example. If there are many more participants, and more shares offered in a market, it has liquidity. Both traders and investors should look for liquid stocks in order to improve their chances of getting good prices in all transactions.

Finally, volatility is a measure of the magnitude of the movement of prices of a stock during a period of time. In this case, bigger does not necessarily mean better. Note there is an absence of market direction in the concept of volatility. That is because volatility can imply down or up moves of the stock. It is important to find stocks that have volatility numbers in accordance with the trading or investing objectives and risk tolerance. It is very frustrating to hold to a stock for long and have it move too little or too much.

Diversifying Your Portfolio

The ideal investment or trading strategy is one that consistently returns profits throughout time. But, as mentioned before, markets don't behave the same for very long. On the contrary, markets are very fluid and tend to alternate between periods of accelerated growth, consolidation and decline.

Everyone has either heard or experienced first-hand the unprecedented rally the stock market had at the end of the 90s, and early 2000. As good as this rally has been, the market has fallen periodically into mediocre or negative moods where it seemed no money was safe in the market. This is not only true for stocks but for every other economical area.

Diversification is one of the most valuable tools to help you fully participate in marketwide rallies, and to safeguard against general market declines.

Diversifying consists of distributing money in different investment and/or trading vehicles that are not directly or inversely correlated. There is a fine line between having too much vested in one or few vehicles, and having capital spread out through too many investments. Falling to either extreme can either produce losses or severely limit potential profits. Diversifying is done with the intention of insuring consistent profits for extended periods of time.

The most important aspect of diversifying is to approach managing capital outside the box even when there is a certain plan of action with great possibilities for potential returns using a particular investment vehicle.

You can increase diversification by not limiting your investments to just stocks. As mentioned before, stocks are an amazing source of opportunities to make profits, but don't forget that there have been, and there will be periods of time in the future, where other investment vehicles will offer greater returns. So don't discount having part of your capital working in other areas like: short-term trading, investing, real estate, bonds, commodities and cash.

When you have diversity by choosing different vehicles, you can also diversify within each vehicle. For example, you can investigate different markets, industry groups and market capitalisations.

Diverse Markets

Diverse markets are those which are open to investment or trade in stocks from different countries, regions and/or exchanges. Stock performance is often influenced by factors local to the country or the region where the stock originates. By choosing stocks from different countries, regions or exchanges you are decreasing the possibilities that these local events or scenarios will affect all or a significant part of your portfolio at the same time.

Many analysts have noted that economic changes and events that are local to a region are now being felt across the world. This sensitivity is commonly attributed to economic globalisation and technology bringing communities, markets and people around the world closer together.

Industry Groups

Every company belongs to an industry where there are peers, competitors, suppliers, governmental agencies, clients etc. Each one of these entities can be called a component of the industry.

The interaction and performance of every company in an industry has a major effect on individual stock. Entire industry groups usually move in synchronicity. They are usually directly correlated, but some subgroups can be inversely correlated as well.

Choosing stocks from different industry groups is one of the most valuable tools in the search for a diverse portfolio. To do this effectively investors need a certain awareness and industry expertise about what sectors can affect or can lead others. For example, a comment from a company that belongs to the semi-conductor industry group about the demand for their materials being lower than expected can greatly affect all chip manufactures because it implies that the chip manufacturers are reducing production levels. This, in turn, affects computer hardware stocks.

Market Capitalisation

Market capitalisation is a great way to both leverage risk and reduce risk in any stock portfolio.

As explained in the Market Capitalisation section of this book, stocks with different size of market capitalisation behave very differently. It is very advisable to own stocks that belong to each of the market capitalisation groups and vary the percentage invested in each group depending on the expected results of the trading strategies.

If the focus of the trading strategy is to have aggressive profits, possibly using trading as a source of income, it is normally recommended to work with a greater percentage of small and mid capitalisation stocks. If the objective is to have long-term growth then focus your studies on large capitalisation stocks.

Again, it is all about achieving balance amongst the stock types in the portfolio while still having it customised to meet the objectives.

News And The Stock Market

There are many news items published every day about particular stocks, but most of them do not seem to have any effect on stock prices.

First of all, you must understand that news items are descriptions of events that happened in the immediate past. News articles or news items will not affect stock prices. The event behind the news item is what will make the stock price move. If you have the intention of using news items to make profits in the stock market, your success will be in direct relation to the time elapsed from the moment the event occurs to the moment you get the news item, read it and act.

To understand how stock prices are related to news items, or vice versa, you need to go back to basics and distinguish what it is that makes the stock prices move. As mentioned repeatedly in this chapter, stock prices oscillate around the agreed fair value of the stock. When the fair value of the stock changes, the stock will go into a rally or a decline until it reaches its new fair value.

To distinguish what news items can signal a potential change in the price of a stock, you need to be savvy enough to discern what news items are describing an event that changes the current or expected fair value of the stock.

When in retrospect you study any news item that marked a significant change in a stock price, you will find that the event described in the news item changed some element of the formulas listed in the Financial Fundamental Analysis section. As a result, the stock suddenly appeared as under- or overvalued.

Let's return to the Qualcom example. For some time Qualcom Inc.'s stock had oscillated around $40/share. Then a news article was released describing how industry experts projected that 70-90% of the mobile devices in the world would be using Qualcom CDMA technology in the next 10-15 years. The expectations of their potential profits, thus their earnings expectations, multiplied about 100 fold. This made the PE Ratio fall dramatically, leaving the stock severely undervalued in comparison with its industry peers and causing one of the most dramatic rallies for a single stock in recent times.

Was it just the news article that caused the rally? Definitely not. This was a news article that was a description of an event that greatly changed the expected fair value of the stock.

Different Types Of News Items

Not all news items will signal a change in stock prices. Different categories can be defined to distinguish what types of news items can be used to make profits with stocks.

The first category divides news into two groups - news items that describe an event that change the financial outlook of the stock, and informational news items that describe events that do not significantly affect the financial outlook of the stock.

There are many news items released as informational or public relations pieces to expand the knowledge of the public or market participants. This is an event that is already known in the market. The event can be a change for the company but doesn't necessarily imply a change in the fundamental financial information. These types of news items have little or no effect on the stock prices.

The second category divides news items in three: news items that announce that an event will occur in the future, news items that announce that an expected event was just completed, and news items that announce events or situations that occurred in the past.

News items that announce that an event will occur in the future are amongst the most common types of news items that can be used for trading and investments. An example is an announcement about an adjustment to future expected profit numbers. Having these numbers rise increases consumer demand.

News items that announce the completion of an event may appear very meaningful, but the market participants were already informed about the event through a previous news item, and the stock already included this event in its price. This is why a company may have record earnings for a quarter but at the moment the earnings are released the stock does not move significantly. This is a give-away sign that the market participants were already expecting these results, thus had already taken action beforehand. This is probably where the common saying amongst traders "buy on the rumour, sell on the news" comes from.

News articles that describe an event that occurred in the past have little or no effect in future performance of the stock. This is the type of news items that will be least useful in your quest to generate profits. As mentioned before, the market is a forward-looking animal and is only moved when something alters the expected future of a company, industry or market.

In conclusion, the news items that are of most value to traders and investors are those who describe an event that will occur in the future, and that have the potential to change the financial outlook of the stock. These are the type of news items you need to look for to guide your trading activity.

Systematic Approach To Trading And Investing

There can be many different approaches to trading and investing that include one or more of all of these techniques. Whatever you choose to do, be consistent!

In the last few decades there have been many breakthroughs in business management in the area of process control and improvement. Amongst these breakthroughs you have many quality assurance philosophies like SPC (Statistical Process Control), Total Quality Management, the ISO movement etc. What all of these management theories have in common is that all business processes need to be standardised, documented and measured.

The objective of standardising, documenting and measuring a process is to be able to evaluate the efficiency and effectiveness of the business, help isolate and improve problem areas, and monitor the performance of the process into the future to detect potential problems early and avoid major negative consequences.

Trading is no different than any other business discipline. And standardising, documenting and measuring the process used to choose your stocks, then buy and sell them, should be seriously considered as a prerequisite to trading. By doing this, it is possible to monitor the performance of the methodology being followed. Also, it gives you the opportunity to find when and where the strategies performance starts to deteriorate, thus giving you the opportunity to fine tune it and solve any potential problems.

Trading has an important advantage over other disciplines - all the historic information of stock prices and company performance is available for study and can be used to evaluate your trading methodology. Any well-defined trading strategy can be run through stock prices to evaluate how this strategy would have performed in the past, which obviously presents a unique opportunity to see the past performance of the strategy without risking any capital. There are a number of software applications and services that allow you to test trading strategies, but be aware that most of the commercial products focus solely on strategies that use price data.

7. Trading Stocks

After all the analysis has been done, it's time to actually buy and sell shares and start following a trading or investing strategy.

It is possible to buy shares directly from a company or corporation, which saves money in transaction fees, but it is very impractical when done for multiple stocks. Brokerage firms make buy and sell transactions easy and almost transparent to their clients.

Brokerage Firms

Brokerage firms are financial institutions that allow their clients to open one or multiple accounts, deposit and withdraw money, and will even lend money to those who qualify, based on their credit history. The main difference between brokerage houses and banking institutions is that brokerage houses allow their customers to buy and sell shares of stocks from whatever exchanges the brokerage firm has access to.

Brokerage firms can usually buy and sell shares of any institution in the country of origin where the brokerage office is physically located, but it has become more common for brokerage firms to have access to multiple international markets.

It's important to be aware that some brokerage firms specialise and only trade in futures, commodities, options, currencies, bonds or other trading instruments. So, when analysing a brokerage house, the first task is to find out if they allow their customers to trade stocks.

Types Of Brokerage Accounts

Brokerage firms have different levels of service and technology available to their customers, ranging from full service brokerage accounts to direct access trading accounts that will give different advantages, and carry different costs when managing your money. Here are the most common types of accounts.

Full Brokerage Service Accounts

When trading through these accounts the client can place all their transactions through a professional broker over the phone or in person, or can manage their transactions by interacting with different automated systems through the telephone or the Internet.

The main difference between the Full Brokerage Service account and the other types is that when you trade through the profession broker, he can make suggestions and comments and even guide clients to opportunities that they might not be aware of. Also, once the trade is placed, the broker will personally see the trade filled and will notify the client of the details of the transaction.

Because of all these interactions with an actual person, Full Brokerage Services have much higher transaction costs than all other accounts. Full Brokerage accounts might have transaction costs as much as 10 times more than discount brokers, but the help and guidance from a pro can be invaluable for novice traders.

These accounts are ideal for investors who don't have the time, or desire, to do their own research, and for traders who prefer personalised professional service as well as quick and efficient responses to their trading orders.

Discount Brokerage Accounts

Discount brokerage accounts are the self-serve/fast food equivalent to Full Service Brokerage accounts. Discount Brokerage accounts were created with individual traders and small trading outfits that don't feel the need to ask for trading advice from a broker to place their orders.

The main form of interaction to place buy and sell orders is usually a Website, or an automated telephone system where clients place their orders directly into the computer system of the brokerage firm.

Interaction between the customers and brokers or staff from the brokerage house is usually limited to problem resolution or technical and customer support. The overhead costs of maintaining a Discount Brokerage firm is much smaller than a Full Service Brokerage firm, and the savings are passed directly to the customers.

Discount Brokerage firms get their name because the transaction costs for their clients are so much smaller than all other accounts. But again, clients have very little or no guidance from their brokerage house in terms of where and how to manage their money, and in some instances the level of service is not as good.

Discount Brokerage accounts are ideal for longer-term traders that don't require extremely fast execution of their trades and are concerned about transaction costs. They are also good for investors that do their own research and make their own decisions about where to place their money.

Direct Access Trading Accounts

These accounts are the latest trend amongst day traders. Day traders are a subcategory of traders that never carry open positions from one day to the next. Furthermore, their trades usually last minutes or, at the most, hours. Because of the nature of their trades they absolutely require the fastest service available for their trading orders.

Direct Access Trading accounts are set up to access the exchanges without any extra intermediaries or middlemen and are all part of electronic computer networks. They are set up to trade through one or more ECN. The time elapsed between placing the trade and receiving the confirmation is usually measured in seconds, instead of minutes or hours as in other types of trading accounts.

Traders that have Direct Access Trading accounts usually know what they are doing and don't need much assistance, so most of the interaction between the client and the brokerage firm will be through computerised systems (the World Wide Web or custom computer networks).

Margin Trading

Brokerage houses also lend money to their clients to allow them to trade larger numbers of shares. This is called margin trading. In most countries stock brokerage services will lend its clients as much as they have in the account. So, if a margin account has $20,000, the client will be able to buy up to $40,000 of stocks.

Margin trading allows traders to leverage their money. For example, $2,500 is enough to buy 100 shares of a $50 stock through a margin account. If the stock increases in price and is sold at $60 a share the trade returns a profit of $1,000. Note that with a 20% increase in the stock price, the trade generates a 40% return on investment. On the other side of this coin margin trading increases the amount of potential losses as well. A 10% drop in the stock means a 20% loss of the capital used for the trade.

Margin trading can also produce very undesirable results when the account suffers generalised losses. Assume a trader has an account with $10,000 total and he buys 200 shares of ABC at $100 per share. This means he is buying a total of $20,000 worth of ABC stock. Assume that ABC stock drops in price to $70 per share. This drop in the stock price produces a $6,000 loss in his account, leaving his account with only $4,000. He is still holding 200 shares of ABC at $70 a share, which represent holdings of $14,000. This is much more than the 50% margin allowed by most brokers.

In instances like this the brokerage firm will issue a Margin Call, which is a request from the broker to the client asking to provide more funds to reach the minimum balance to support the account. Brokerage firms have a grace period for their clients to provide the additional funds, but if the client does not respond to the request the brokerage firm usually sells all or part of the shares to return the account to balance.

Opening A Brokerage Account

Brokerage accounts are very similar to bank accounts, and brokerage houses have very similar requirements to banks. As a general rule, brokerage houses will first request from their clients identification information, address and contact information. Then they run a financial credit check and, in some instances, a more general background check to ensure their financial safety. Once these credit and background checks are passed to the satisfaction of the brokerage house, the client forwards the funds to the new account and begins placing their orders to buy and sell.

Specific requirements and procedures vary greatly from country to country, and even from brokerage house to brokerage house, but be assured that it is a simple procedure and that the brokerage house really wants you to use them for your trading, so you can expect them to help you with the process.

Types Of Orders

The most common way to make profits with stocks, and the one everyone knows about is to buy a security and, at a later time, sell it at a higher price for a profit. In the trading and investing world this is also called going long, or having a long position in a stock.

In the world of finances, it's not necessary to sit on the sidelines or lose part of those hard-earned profits when the market falls. Just like there are long positions, there are short positions as well. Short positions allow market traders and investors to make profits when the market drops.

A short position, aka short selling, is equivalent to selling a borrowed item, in this case shares, expecting the price to drop in order to buy back this item (or one just like it) for a profit to then return it to the original owner. The process of buying the shares back is also called covering a short position. For investors and traders, the process of borrowing the stock, and returning it to the owner is completely transparent. The brokerage house is responsible for finding shares for investors or traders to borrow, and ultimately covers the position. All their clients have to do is place the orders to sell and then buy back.

Short selling has not been a very popular tool to make profits in the last few decades, mainly because the world economy has been in a general up trend. Because of this, short selling has become a tool for short-term traders to make profits when speculating about declining prices of a stock or the market.

Short selling might feel like a novel idea, but don't get too exited about the prospects from it. Mathematically, there is only so much profits to be made from short selling because the price of stocks can't actually go to negative numbers. To illustrate this, let's use ABC stock. If someone bought 100 shares ABC very early on, they would have had a return on their investment of several thousands of percentage points. If a second investor timed the market perfectly to sell and then buy 100 shares of ABC, the most profit he could have ever made is approximately $7,000.

The standard terms for opening and closing positions are: buying, selling to close, selling short and buying to cover/buying to close. For each one of these orders there are also three major variations, which can give you additional precision when trading or investing. These are market, stop and limit orders.

Market orders are the easiest to understand. Market orders simply mean to buy or sell as soon as possible at the best possible price. These orders are usually the fastest to be filled, as they have no criteria to follow. If the market order is a buy it will be matched with the seller that has the best price regardless of what their price might be.

Market orders allow for potential slippage. Slippage is defined as the difference in price from the moment an order is placed to the price where the order is actually filled. So, if stock ABC is trading at $50 per share and a trader places a market order to buy 500 shares, which is filled 2 minutes later at a price of $51 per share, then they had a $1 slippage. In this particular trade they lost the opportunity to profit from $500. Slippage becomes more and more significant when trading high numbers of shares.

A way to help avoid slippage is by using stop and limit orders. Stop and limit orders are special types of orders where a minimum, or maximum price is required for the trade to be filled. A limit order can be 'buy 100 shares of ABC at $70 limit.' This means that this trader will buy 100 shares of ABC at $70 or any lower price. It's important to note that because these orders are conditional to the price of the stock reaching a certain price, these orders might never get filled at all.

Limit orders are usually thought of as the specified price 'or better.' As shown in the last example, when buying shares limit orders force the trade to be at the specified price or lower. When selling shares, limit orders force the trade to be at the specified price or higher. Limit orders are usually used to open a position. In other words, to buy or sell short.

The reverse applies to stop orders. Stop orders can be though of as 'or worse' orders. When an order is placed to 'sell 100 shares of ABC at $65 stop' the trader will sell 100 shares of ABC only if the stock drops to $65 per share or lower. (Note, if you buy shares with a stop order it is interpreted as the specified price or higher.) Stop orders are usually used as the last line of protection to avoid having losses become unmanageable. It's very common in the industry to have a stop loss strategy which usually includes stop orders.

Here are the different types of orders available to trade the markets:

	Stop	Limit
Buy	or higher	or lower
Sell to Close	or lower	or higher
Sell Short	or lower	or higher
Buy to Close	or higher	or lower

8. Alternatives To Investing In Stock Shares

Buying and selling stock shares is not the only way to participate in the stock market. There are other financial vehicles derived from stocks that allow for participation in the stock market. The two most commonly used are Stock Options and Mutual Funds.

Stock Options

Stock options are contracts between two parties regarding a transaction involving stocks. Stock options give the right, but not the obligation, to buy or sell a stock at a specific price before an agreed upon date.

The party that owns the stock shares, and is granting the option, is usually called the writer of the option contract. This party receives a premium paid for the contract up front.

There are two types of options: calls and puts. Calls give you the option to buy a certain number of shares at a specified price, and puts give you the option to sell short. Stock options are specific to one stock, which is called the underlying security. The specified price at which you are allowed to buy or sell short the shares of the underlying stock is called the strike price. The expiration date is the day when the contract becomes void or expires. Usually it corresponds to the third Friday of a specific month. The receiver of the contract has the option to act on or before this day, or to let the contract expire worthless. And finally, every contract gives the rights to 100 shares of the underlying stock.

For example, assume it's early January of the year 2002, and ABC is trading at approximately $80 per share. John Doe enters an option contract with the specifics '85 March 2002 Call' and he pays $300 of premium for this contract. John Doe has gained the option to buy 100 shares of ABC at $85 per share before the third Friday of March 2002.

John Doe is counting on the price of ABC shares not only to be over 85$, but to be over $88 by the time of expiration of the option contract or earlier. If ABC is at $95 per share at the time of expiration, Mr Doe can buy the 100 shares at $85, and either hold the position with an instant 10-point profit, or sell the shares at market value. But why is $88 the break-even price for this transaction? The reason is because of the premium Mr Doe paid for the option up front. He paid $300 for one contract that controls 100 shares, so he needs 3 extra points above the strike price to break even. Any price over $88 per share would mean profits for Mr Doe. If the stock price of ABC does not surpass the strike price, $85 in this example, the writer of the stock gets to keep the $300 premium as profits.

Benefits Of Trading Options

The greatest advantage of trading options is giving traders an amazing increase in leverage. In the previous example, you saw how with only $300 up front, John Doe could have had a $700 return if ABC stock rallied up 10 points in a two-month time period. On the other hand, if John Doe were trading stock shares directly, he would have had to commit $8,500 to the transaction to get $1,000 in return. It is obvious which method gives the better return on investment.

As usual, greater profit potential comes along with greater risk. Even if ABC increased from $80 to $85 per share, the option contract would be worthless at the expiration date in March and John Doe would loose all his investment in this particular transaction. A different way of saying this is that the option game involves time. Knowing how to account for time is a huge component of option strategies and, if time runs out, the investment can be completely lost. In comparison, stock investors can almost disregard time in their analysis and focus on studying financial and price information.

More About Calls And Puts

When trading calls and puts, buying or selling shares of the underlying security doesn't have to be the only outcome. Calls and puts are priced according to a number of factors, and just like you buy and sell shares of a particular security you can also buy and sell option contracts.

Option contracts are priced according to four major factors: the strike price of the option contract, the price of the underlying security, the remaining time to expiration of the contract and the volatility of the underlying stock.

The price of the option contract and its relation to the underlying price are the most obvious of factors that affect option contract pricing. For calls, the higher the stock price the higher the price of the option contract and, if at any point the stock price is greater than the strike price, the option contract is said to have intrinsic value. If a stock is trading at $60 per share, the intrinsic value of all '$50 March Calls' is $10. If the stock price is under the strike price the intrinsic value is said to be zero.

Then there is time to expiration and volatility. The amount of time left until the expiration of the option influences the pricing of an option contract. In options, more time until expiration means greater probabilities of the stock price surpassing the strike price and increasing its intrinsic value. Because of this, traders will pay higher prices for options that have more time left until expiration date. Alternatively, as option contracts run out of time their value decreases exponentially until it reaches zero after expiration day.

Related to the expiration date is the volatility of the underlying security. Volatility is a measure of the magnitude of the movement of prices of a stock during a period of time. If the stock prices are steady it is irrelevant if there is a lot of time until the expiration day. So the greater the volatility of the underlying security, the greater the value of the option contracts as well.

In light of all this, many traders do not wait until expiration or even exercise their options. Instead they make profits buying and selling option contracts, just as others focus on buying and selling shares.

If you buy an option contract for $300, and the price or volatility of the underlying symbol increases significantly, then there might be an opportunity to sell the option contracts in the market for a profit. As mentioned, option contracts change in value daily, so the contract purchased at $300 can be sold a few days later at $500 for a profit. Still, be wary of time, as with each day that passes there is less time available until expiration, and the value of option contracts fall exponentially in regard to time.

Writing Versus Buying Calls And Puts

Yet another alternative to play the options game is to write option contracts, also called granting options.

An option contract writer gives another the option to buy from them a predetermined number of shares, at a specific price before an agreed-upon time. The reason to do this is to get the premium in advance.

When a trader grants option contracts he is assuming the stock price will not reach the strike price, and that the option will expire worthless to the holder of the options. For an option writer, all the factors are completely reversed.

Time becomes the option writer's biggest ally. As time elapses the value of the option decreases and the probabilities of the option being exercised at expiration decrease exponentially.

Movement in price and volatility become foes, because the greater the stock price changes, the greater the possibilities of the option being exercised.

Writing option contracts is a great way of immediately obtaining funds for other purposes, but it is not the best strategy for creating significant profits.

When a trader buys calls or puts, the potential profit is unlimited, and the potential maximal loss is the price paid for the option. Writers of options have a maximum profit equal to the price of the option, and unlimited loss potential.

Writing options can be a very dangerous strategy in volatile markets and is usually done by advanced traders that have strategies to minimise their risk.

Hedging Positions With Options

You can also create a strategy to use your stock options in conjunction with your stock holdings. The most common version of this is hedging your stock positions with options.

Hedging a stock position with options involves buying shares AND put options for the same stock at the same time, or selling short shares and buying call options.

Buying shares and put options can serve to limit your losses and give you unlimited profit potential, lessening the considerations and worry about time.

This works by buying certain amount of shares, and a few put option contracts that have a strike price under the current price. If the stock rallies to the upside, the stock shares will generate your profits. Given that options have limited risk, the maximum loss incurred is the price paid for the options, which can be considered part of the transaction costs. If the stock falls the put contracts will increase in value and will serve as a way to offset the losses of the stock until the stock recovers or the position is closed.

This can be a very powerful technique that can save much capital, but it is usually done with large transactions where the cost of the option contracts will not significantly impact the overall profit of the transactions.

Mutual Funds

A mutual fund is simply a collection of stocks and/or bonds. This collection of stocks and/or bonds is usually managed by a professional mutual funds manager to actively buy and sell stocks or bonds for the fund. Through a yearly fee, the mutual funds shareholders finance the operation of the fund.

The main advantages of mutual funds are that investors have a full-time manager actively looking after the fund, and they provide instant diversification because investors that buy shares of a fund effectively hold several different companies. Also, because of the diversification, severe drops in one or more of the stocks belonging to the fund will usually not significantly affect the overall performance of the fund. This is normally called dilution of investments, and it is commonly listed as both an advantage and disadvantage of mutual funds. Many funds have small holdings on many different stocks and bonds, which reduces the impact that a few star performers might have on the fund. This means the overall value of the fund moves up slowly and gradually. Another disadvantage is additional costs. Many mutual funds have a few costs that are not mentioned in much of the literature of the funds, but end up eating profits nonetheless.

Though you would think that mutual funds provide great benefits to shareholders through professional money managers and diversification, it is estimated that only 20% of funds will outperform the stock markets' overall average returns. The average mutual fund returns approximately 2% less per year to its shareholders than does the stock market, and the average gross returns of funds matches the 11% performance posted by the market in the last few years. It is believed that the main reason mutual funds underperform the market is the costs and overhead associated with maintaining it. And remember, there are still 20% of funds that do outperform your average returns. Still, for new investors, it is advisable to start by buying an index fund. Let's study the different types of funds next.

Types Of Funds

Mutual funds have become a very popular investment vehicle, especially thanks to the boom in the stock market. As interest in mutual funds has increased in the last few years, so have the different types of funds. Here is a list of the most common ones:

Bond Funds

Bond mutual funds are pooled amounts of money invested in bonds. Bonds are debt letters issued by companies or governments. Someone who buys bonds is lending money to the company or government that issued the bond, and will usually collect regular interest payments until the money is returned. Usually the interest paid by the issuers is a set percentage, thus bonds are usually categorised as fixed-income investments.

Balanced Funds

These are made of a mix between stocks and bonds. Depending on the fund manager and the strategy they are following, the percentage of the fund dedicated to each group can vary. Normally around half or more of the funds are dedicated to holding stocks. It is always important to know the distribution between stocks and bonds to know the risk/reward/possibility of success ratio for these types of funds.

Equity Funds

Stock or equity mutual funds are pooled amounts of money that are only invested in stocks. Many mutual funds invest solely in stocks according to their market capitalisation. For example, there are funds that specialise in growth stocks and are put together from small and mid cap stocks. Other funds try to have different mixes between the three market capitalisation categories searching for balance. Another form of general equity funds are called index funds. Index funds are funds that mirror one of the market indices like the S&P 500 or the Dow 30. As mentioned earlier, approximately 80% of funds underperform the average market return, and the average market return is a reference to the major indices. Because they are simple to manage, costs of these funds are usually much lower. Index funds have beaten over 80% of other funds in the last few years, so it is a great place to start your mutual funds investments as you try to find the top 15% performers, whomever they might be.

Sector Funds

These funds invest in one particular sector of the economy like technology, finance, computers, the Internet, biotechnology etc. Sector funds can be extremely volatile, or extremely slow moving, because economic sectors periodically oscillate from very attractive to unattractive.

Using Mutual Funds And Stocks In Your Portfolio

It is wise to diversify holdings by using different investment vehicles throughout a portfolio, but always remember that mutual funds are a collection of stocks and sometimes bonds that are put together by a mutual fund manager.

It is possible to overload your portfolio with one stock if one or more of the mutual funds in your portfolio also have this stock. For example, if you have 500 shares of ABC and you have two mutual funds that have ABC as a significant component of the portfolio, you will be effectively loading your portfolio with ABC stock. This can be a blessing if ABC does well and continues to dominate the software market, but if the company falters in any way your entire portfolio might be compromised because you have too many eggs in one basket.

Another possible pitfall is to have two mutual funds in your portfolio that have stocks that are inversely correlated. This can happen in a market where there are strong competitors or any other circumstance where stocks are inversely correlated, so when one rises the other falls, and vice versa. If this happens, these stocks can cancel out each other's profits.

Fund Fees

Mutual funds charge fees. Through these fees they cover their expenses and manage to make profits. The most important fee to understand is the mutual fund's expense ratio. The expense ration is composed of several sub-fees.

The investment advisory fee, or management fee, is the money used to pay the manager(s) of the mutual fund. On average this fee oscillates around 1% of the annual fund assets, and is necessary to keep the fund manager on board.

Administrative costs are the costs of record keeping, mailings, customer service, offices etc. Needless to say, these are all important costs that can vary greatly from fund to fund. Most Administrative Costs vary between 0.2% and 0.5% of the annual fund assets.

The 12b-1 distribution fee is usually under 1% of the fund's assets and is used on marketing and advertising, and distribution services. So with the 12b-1 fee, investors are contributing for commercials, and other marketing and promotional ventures for the fund.

It is not of great concern to investors how these fees are distributed, but it is important to find how much the expense ratio is. Remember that the returns of the average funds in the last few years are about 2% under the overall market and the average fund also has an expense ratio of about 1.5%.

Another advantage of the index funds, mentioned earlier, is that the expense ratio is typically less than 0.5% because they are much easier to maintain.

Fund Loads

Load refers to the sales charge many funds use to compensate the broker for their services in selling the fund to an investor. Fund loads can be thought of as additional costs the investor will incur when buying a fund.

No-load funds are simply those that are sold directly to the investor, rather than through a middleman. In recent years there has been an explosion of no-load funds in parallel to the proliferation of discount brokers in the stock market. So, currently, it does not make much sense to choose load funds, unless the performance is extraordinary and clearly superior to other funds.

There are a few different types of load funds, amongst the most popular are:

Front-End Load

These funds charge a commission up front when you buy shares in the fund. These commissions usually go directly to the broker or company that sell you the fund, and can usually range from 5% to 9% of your investment.

Deferred Load Funds

These funds are also called contingent deferred sale load (CDSL) funds, and sometimes are called back-end loads). These funds defer the fee to when the investor sells, or leaves the fund but on average they have the same range as the front-end load funds.

Level Load Funds

These funds usually charge much smaller front loads, but they charge a level load every year thereafter. Although these may look more attractive (cost-wise) than the prior two, if they are held for a long period of time they usually end up being more expensive because of the annual level load.

Load Vs. No-Load

If you are savvy enough to make your own trading and investment decisions regarding stocks, you don't need help making decisions about your mutual funds and you don't need load funds. It would be better to take on an advisor to help you make decisions in exchange for a commission. Other than that, it has been shown in several research papers that load and no-load do not make mutual funds better or worse - they perform the same either way.

Selecting Funds

Selecting mutual funds is a process somewhat different to selecting stocks. You must first consider what funds align themselves with your objectives as an investor. Some funds play with risk and reward to provide better performance by taking more risks, while others go for long-term growth with lower risk. This information is always readily available in the fund prospectus.

Research the past performance of the fund. This is a great way to find consistent winners, and all funds readily provide this information. Look to see if the fund specialised in a specific market or industry group, and research that market or industry group and the expected performance. Most markets are cyclical, so now might or might not be the right time to jump into a fund that is specialised in a particular industry group.

As explained in the costs and load sections, take a serious look at the costs for a specific fund. Regardless of performance, costs and loads might bring down the performance of the fund as much as 8% to 10% of the capital you invest.

Look at turnover rates. A fund's turnover rate represents the percentage of holdings that it changes every year. Managed mutual funds have an average turnover rate of 80%. This means these funds sell most of their holdings every year and hence incur large brokerage commissions to buy and sell stocks. Also, funds with a large rotation of holdings usually distribute capital gains yearly to the shareholders, which are taxed at much higher percentages than long-term investments. This can also seriously cut into the investor's profits. Some funds, especially index funds, can have turnover rates as low as 10%.

Finally, always review the Prospectus of the fund. The Prospectus has most, if not all, the information you need to size up a mutual fund and decide if it is worth your valuable investment capital.

9. Trading Dos And Don'ts

There are many dos and don'ts lists in the investment and trading world - some dos on one list even change to don'ts in others - but don't despair. Most of the confusion is caused because it is not made clear who the advice is for. When reading or hearing about financial markets it is necessary to clearly identify whether the information is aimed at traders or investors, because strategies and sound advice for one group might be harmful for the other.

Here are some dos and don'ts that can serve all:

Develop a methodology, or strategy, that you can follow consistently. This will allow you to measure your results, and identify what works and what does not

Diversify! Don't fill your portfolio with stocks from one industry group, or with so few stocks that you don't profit when the market starts to rise.

Do your research. Look into the stocks, funds and option contracts for fundamental information, price data and relevant news.

Don't follow rumours or chatrooms. You might find a few good trades in chatrooms and from rumours, but it is simply not possible to have reliable consistent results by going down this road.

Don't hold on just because you have to be right. If you do your research and jump into a position where your assumptions were simply not accurate, get out of it and look for the next opportunity. Holding on to a position when your reasons have been proven incorrect is similar to playing the lottery: you are just waiting for something to happen to save your trade and your pride!

Always have a stop loss in place. A stop loss is an order that takes you out of a position before losses start becoming unbearable.

10. Reference Materials

Fortunately, much has been written and published about stocks. Actually, there has been enough published that a common pitfall of starting investors and traders is to attempt to read it all before jumping into the game: "After all, this is MY money we are talking about!" is a very common sentence I have heard from many that dedicate months and sometimes years studying before taking the jump.

The World Wide Web has become a rich resource of information about trading and current events. It is a medium through which real-time information is distributed to individuals and organisations throughout the entire world. It is also the main medium through which individual investors and traders interact with their brokers.

There follows a list of references, both on the web and in print, for you to further your education on stocks, trading and investing. But remember, don't try to read it all to stop yourself getting started in the markets.

Internet Resources

General Information Sites

These sites have general information, educational and sometimes opinionated articles about the markets, trading and investing.

US Markets

http://moneycentral.msn.com/investor/home.asp - ABC's Money Central for Investors. This is a very robust site, which is mainly dedicated to providing news, articles and some price data for investors of US markets. They also have an outstanding Stock Search application called Stock Screener, and a very decent online community of investors.

http://finance.yahoo.com - Yahoo has become one of the most popular sites to get stock related financial information. This site provides extensive up-to-date fundamental financial information, price data and charts, and up-to-the-minute news about any stock in the US market. They also host the most popular message boards specialising in individual stocks, sectors or the market in general.

www.fool.com - The Motley Fool has become an industry favourite thanks to its light-hearted, yet very consistent and to the point, investing advice. This is also a very robust site for investors of US markets where it is easy to find articles about trading strategies, and a very active and opinionated community of investors. Highly recommended for beginners and intermediate investors.

www.cnnfn.com/markets/ - CNNfn.com is the online version of this popular US financial television channel. Its focus is in world, corporate and financial news. There are also daily articles and commentary by industry experts about current market conditions. And of course, up-to-date fundamental and price information for all US stocks.

www.cnbc.com - A very similar site to CNNfn, only it has richer features. In addition to what CNNfn offers, it has a decent stock screener which helps find stocks that meet your criteria. And it has a respectable online community, most of whom are viewers of the parent television channel.

http://quicken.aol.com/investments/mutualfunds - Search engine that will provide expense ratios and other financial information about most US mutual funds.

www.Quicken.com - Great personal financial information from the creators of the software application Quicken, and it has valuable information about mutual funds.

www.fundstyle.com - Specialises in information about US-based mutual funds

www.smartmoney.com - Has a section dedicated to mutual funds.

Europe & World

http://uk.finance.yahoo.com/ - Like the main Yahoo finance page, only it specialises in the UK markets, and links to Yahoo sites for the major markets in Europe and the world.

http://de.finance.yahoo.com/ - The German version of the Yahoo finance page. I'm sure you are getting the picture of the Yahoo financial services.

www.fste.com - FTSE is a financial institution whose main purpose is to create, update and publish worldwide financial indices. This site has all the information about, and the actual current and historical data, for all FTSE indices. These are very popular indices that are used when trying to determine market direction. It is partially owned by the London Stock Exchange, thus it specialises in European indices, and its most popular index is the FTSE 100.

www.gsionline.com/exchange.htm - GSI is a research firm that specialise in finding information about any stock, any exchange, anywhere in the world. They find financial fundamental, and government and regulatory documents and information that are not readily available to the general public.

www.bloomberg.com - Bloomberg is easily one of the largest international financial institutions in the world. Accordingly, this is an enormous site with financial information of virtually all markets in the world. It specialises in up-to-the-minute news and price data of any trading instrument worldwide, and includes everything from an online university to message boards.

www.investorwords.com - This site has an impressive glossary of over 5,000 investor terms organised both alphabetically and by topic.

Technical Analysis Sites

These sites either have information, online tools or products that will aid you in the research and study of technical analysis of stock prices.

www.traders.com - Traders.com is the online version of *Stock And Commodities* magazine, which is one of the most popular stock trading magazines in the United States. It has heavily researched articles by industry experts. Both the magazine and the Website are highly recommended for anyone interested in technical analysis.

www.tradestation.com - TradeStation Technologies has been for many years the leader in technical analysis tools. You will not find any articles or information about trading on the Website, but you will be able to subscribe to the most powerful commercial Internet service dedicated to technical analysis of stocks and commodities.

www.equis.com - Equis.com is the producer of the software application Metastock, which has also been a leader for many years in software applications for investors and traders. On the Website you will find information regarding the markets, including a very valuable resource for technical analysis enthusiasts: a free electronic version of the book *Technical Analysis From A To Z* by Steven Achiles.

Exchanges

Exchanges are organised market places where buying and selling take place. These sites have information about the major exchanges, who they are and what services and products they offer.

US Stock Exchanges

www.nasdaq.com - The US NASDAQ exchange

www.nyse.com - The US New York Stock Exchange

www.amex.com - The US AMEX exchange

European Stock Exchanges

www.londonstockexchange.com - The UK London Stock Exchange

http://deutsche-boerse.com/ - The German Bourse Group

www.borsaitalia.it/ - The Italian Borsa

Full Brokerage Houses

Full Brokerage Houses offer the ability to place trades, and have professionals that offer trading advice and guidance to manage your stock portfolio. In essence, they not only perform brokerage functions but also have available a host of other services related to trading and managing your money. Remember that the point of using a Full Brokerage service is to actually talk to professionals to get support, so don't limit yourself to trading online with these companies.

US Brokers

www.schwab.com/ - Charles Schwab has built a powerhouse in the financial industry, and their services are amongst the most complete in the industry.

www.mldirect.ml.com - Merril Linch is another powerhouse in the financial industry. Similar to Schwab, they have been servicing a major share of the financial market for quite some time.

http://finance.americanexpress.com/finance/brokerage.asp - From the famous credit card company. This is a branch of their financial services arm that offers full brokerage services for US securities.

European Brokers

www.schwab-worldwide.com/Europe/ - This site belongs to the branch of Schwab that specialises in the European market.

www.mlhsbc.co.uk/ - This Merril Linch site lists the services and contact information for Merril Linch UK.

Discount Brokerage Houses

There are many discount brokerage houses in the United States, Europe and the rest of the world, and not all of them offer great services. Before using any of these brokerage houses do your research and enquire about customer satisfaction.

US Discount Brokers

www.datek.com - Datek is one of the most popular discount brokers in the United States. Datek owns the ISLAND ECN, and has the ECN data available through this page.

www.ameritrade.com - The address of another of the most popular discount brokerage houses in the United States

www.suretrade.com - Popular discount brokerage firm.

www.scottrade.com - Popular discount brokerage firm.

www.tdwaterhouse.com - Popular discount brokerage firm.

European Discount Brokers

www.europeanbrokerno1.com - This site, and the accompanying brokerage house, is the result of the merger between DAB Bank and SelfTrade.com. This new brokerage house claims to be the largest brokerage service in Europe.

www.directinvest.co.uk - This site is from Direct Invest in the United Kingdom. They offer discount brokerage services in the UK.

www.dljDirect.co.uk - This site belongs to a branch of the US brokerage firm DLJ Direct, and specialises in providing trading services to the UK.

www.financial-discounts.co.uk - Popular discount brokerage firm in the UK

www.tdwaterhouse.co.uk - This site belongs to a branch of the US brokerage firm TD Waterhouse, and specialises in providing trading services to the UK.

Direct Access Trading

Direct access trading is relatively new technology directed at day traders. By using direct access trading it is possible to tap directly into the exchange by placing orders through one or more ECNs. Execution of trades and confirmations are reported in seconds, and they are currently the most effective brokerage service for day traders to improve their execution times.

www.cybertrader.com - Cybertrader is a direct access broker that was acquired a few years ago by Schwab Investment services to tap into the day trading business.

www.tradestation.com - New service at the time of publication of this book.

Books

One Up On Wall Street: How To Use What You Already Know To Make Money In The Market by Peter Lynch & John Rothchild, April 2000. Publicly-acclaimed book by Peter Lynch, one of the undisputed stars of the stock market in the last few decades.

The Motley Fool's Investing Without A Silver Spoon: How Anyone Can Build Wealth Through Direct Investing by Jeff Fischer & David Gardner, August 1999. This book propelled Jeff Fischer and David Gardner into financial fame. It is written with much investment savvy and a light-hearted approach that has made it, and the Website www.fool.com, a personal favourite.

The Motley Fool Investment Guide: How The Fool Beats Wall Street's Wise Men And How You Can Too by David Gardner & Tom Gardner, January 1996. Another great book to get started with serious investing strategies.

Great Companies, Great Returns by Jim Huguet, September 1999. Great book explaining Mr Huguet's approach to long-term investing.

Technical Analysis Of Stock Trends by Robert D Edwards & John F Magee, May 1997. This is a classic textbook for stock evaluation. Often referred to as the Bible of technical analysis, a must for traders and investors interested in technical analysis.

The Visual Investor: How To Spot Market Trends by John J Murphy & John L Murphy, October 1996. John L Murphy is a recognised expert who specialises in technical analysis. For many years he participated in many stock market-related programs on CNBC. Excellent introductory book for technical analysis enthusiasts.

Technical Analysis Explained: The Successful Investor's Guide To Spotting Investment Trends And Turning Points by Martin J Pring, June 1991. This is another classic that gives a thorough introduction to technical analysis for investors, it's a great source to set your technical analysis foundation.

The Technical Analysis Of Stocks, Options & Futures by William F Eng, May 1988. Well-rounded book about technical analysis that covers many different approaches to studying price movement of Stocks, Options and Futures.

The New Market Wizards by Jack Schwager, January 1992. Mr Schwager interviews many of the top traders, giving amazing insights into what it takes to succeed in the trading world.

Common Sense On Mutual Funds: New Imperatives For The Intelligent Investor by John C Bogle & Peter L Bernstein, December 2000. Great book where Mr Bogle shares invaluable insights about investment and mutual funds.

Mutual Funds For Dummies by Eric Tyson & James C Collins, 3rd Ed, April 2001. A great book that explains all you need to get started with mutual funds in a very entertaining format.

11. Glossary

There are many resources online that can serve as invaluable glossaries to learn about trading and investing terminology. One of the most thorough is www.investorwords.com which has more than 50,000 industry-related terms. Here are a few useful terms.

At-The-Money Option: An option with a strike price that is equal, or nearly equal, to the current market price of the underlying stock.

Ask: Price at which a stock is being sold at a specific market.

Bar Chart: A chart that graphs the high, low and settlement prices for a specific trading session over a given period of time.

Bear Market: A time period of declining market prices.

Bid: Offered buying price for a stock or option contract at a specific market.

Broker: A company or individual that executes stock and options orders on behalf of financial and commercial institutions and/or individual investors and traders.

Bull Market: A time period of rising market prices.

Call Option: An option that gives the buyer the right, but not the obligation, to purchase the underlying stock at the strike price on or before the expiration date.

Cancelling Order: An order that deletes a customer's previous order.

Charting: The use of charts to analyse market behaviour. Those who use charting as a trading method plot such factors as: high, low and closing prices; average price movements; volume; and open interest.

Commission Fee: A fee charged by a broker for executing a transaction. Also referred to as brokerage fee.

Consumer Price Index (CPI): A major inflation measure computed by the US Department of Commerce. It measures the change in prices of a fixed market basket of some 385 goods and services in the previous month.

Day Traders: Speculators who take positions in stocks, options or future contracts and liquidate them prior to the close of the same trading day.

Econometrics: The application of statistical and mathematical methods in the field of economics to test and quantify economic theories and the solutions to economic problems.

Exercise: The action taken by the holder of a call option if they wish to purchase the underlying futures contract, or by the holder of a put option if they wish to sell the underlying futures contract.

Expiration Date: Date after which an option contract will be voided, or expired. Options on stocks generally expire on the third Friday of the expiration month.

Floor Broker: An individual who executes orders for the purchase or sale of any stocks or option contracts for any other individual or institution.

Floor Trader: An individual who executes trades for the purchase or sale of any stock or option contracts for their individual account, or the account of the firm they represent.

Fundamental Financial Analysis: Study of financial information about a stock to evaluate the overall economic health of the corporation.

High: The highest price of the day for a particular stock or option contract.

In-The-Money Option: An option having intrinsic value. A call option is in-the-money if its strike price is below the current price of the underlying futures contract. A put option is in-the-money if its strike price is above the current price of the underlying futures contract. See Intrinsic Value.

Intrinsic Value: The amount by which an option is in-the-money. See In-the-Money Option

Limit Order: An order where the customer sets a limit on the price and/or time of execution.

Liquidity: A characteristic of a security, option or market with enough units outstanding to allow large transactions without a substantial change in price. Institutional investors are inclined to seek out liquid markets for investments so that their trading activity will not significantly influence the market price.

Low: The lowest price of the day for a particular stock or option contract.

Margin Call: A call from a clearing house to a clearing member, or from a brokerage firm to a customer, to bring margin deposits up to a required minimum level.

Market Order: An order to buy or sell stock or option contracts, to be filled at the best possible price and as soon as possible.

Moving Averages: A statistical price analysis method intended to identify price trends. A moving average is calculated by adding the prices for a predetermined number of days and then dividing by the number of days.

Offer: An expression indicating one's desire to sell a stock or option contract at a given price; the opposite of bid. Also called Ask.

Open Interest: The total number of option contracts of a given stock that have not yet been offset by an opposite option transaction nor fulfilled by the option exercise. Each open transaction has a buyer and a seller, but for calculation of open interest only one side of the contract is counted.

Option: A contract that conveys the right, but not the obligation, to buy or sell a particular item at a certain price for a limited time. Only the seller of the option is obligated to perform.

Option Buyer: The purchaser of either a call or put option. Option buyers receive the right, but not the obligation, to buy or sell a predetermined number of stocks. Also referred to as the holder.

Option Premium: The price of an option. The sum of money the option buyer pays and the option seller receives for the rights granted by the option.

Option Seller: The person who sells an option in return for a premium and is obligated to perform when the holder exercises their right under the option contract. Also referred to as the writer.

Out-Of-The-Money Option: An option with no intrinsic value, i.e. a call whose strike price is above the current stock price or a put whose strike price is below the current stock price.

Position: A market commitment. A buyer is said to have a long position and, conversely, a short seller is said to have a short position.

Position Trader: An approach to trading in which the trader either buys or sells securities and holds them for an extended period of time. Sometimes called investors.

Put Option: An option that gives the option buyer the right but not the obligation to sell (go short) the underlying stock at the strike price on or before the expiration date.

Range (Price): The distance between the highest and the lowest price traded during a given trading session, week, month, year etc.

Resistance: A level above which prices have difficulty penetrating.

Secondary Market: Market where previously-issued securities are bought and sold.

Security: Common or preferred stock. A bond of a corporation or government.

Short position: When shares of a stock are sold by an individual or organisation that does not own the stock. This is done when the price is expected to decline, at which point the shares will be bought back for a profit. The act of buying back shares is also called 'covering a short position.'

Speculator: A market participant who tries to profit from buying and selling stock and option contracts by anticipating future price movements. Speculators assume market price risk, and add liquidity and capital to the stock market.

Stock Index: An indicator used to measure and report value changes in a selected group of stocks. How a particular stock index tracks the market depends on its composition. It can, for example, sample stocks, weight individual stocks and use different averaging methods to establish an index.

Stock Market: A market in which shares of stock are bought and sold.

Stop Limit Order: A variation of a stop order in which a trade must be executed at the exact price or better. If the order cannot be executed, it is held until the stated price or better is reached again.

Stop Order: An order to buy or sell when the market reaches a specified point. A stop order to buy becomes a market order when the stock price (or bid) reaches or exceeds the specified price. A stop order to sell becomes a market order when the stock price (or ask) falls below the stop price.

Strike Price: The price at which the stock shares of a call can be purchased, or of a put option can be sold. Also referred to as exercise price.

Support: The price where there is enough interest from buyers to halt a price decline.

Technical Analysis: Study of price data of stocks to find past and current market patterns.

Time Value: The amount of money option buyers are willing to pay for an option in the anticipation that over time, a change in the underlying stock price will cause the option to increase in value. In general, an option premium is the sum of time value and intrinsic value.

Volatility: A measurement of the change in price over a given period. It is often expressed as a percentage and computed as the annual standard deviation of the percentage change in daily price.

Volume: The number of purchases or sales of a stock shares made during a specific period of time. Often the total transactions for one trading day.

The Essential Library

Conspiracy Theories by Robin Ramsay, £3.99

Do you think the X-Files is fiction? That Elvis is dead? That the US actually went to the moon? And don't know that the ruling elite did a deal with the extra-terrestrials after the Roswell crash in 1947... At one time, you could blame the world's troubles on the Masons or the Illuminati, or the Jews, or One Worlders, or the Great Communist Conspiracy. Now we also have the alien-US elite conspiracy, or the alien shape-shifting reptile conspiracy to worry about - and there are books to prove it as well! This book tries to sort out the handful of wheat from the choking clouds of intellectual chaff. For among the nonsensical Conspiracy Theory rubbish currently proliferating on the Internet, there are important nuggets of real research about real conspiracies waiting to be mined.

Ancient Greece by Mike Paine, £3.99

Western civilization began with the Greeks. From the highpoint of the 5th century BC through the cultural triumphs of the Alexandrian era to their impact on the developing Roman empire, the Greeks shaped the philosophy, art, architecture and literature of the Mediterranean world. Mike Paine provides a concise and well-informed narrative of many centuries of Greek history. He highlights the careers of great political and military leaders like Pericles and Alexander the Great, and shows the importance of the great philosophers like Plato and Aristotle. Dramatists and demagogues, stoics and epicureans, aristocrats and helots take their places in the unfolding story of the Greek achievement.

Black Death by Sean Martin, £3.99

The Black Death is the name most commonly given to the pandemic of bubonic plague that ravaged the medieval world in the late 1340s. From Central Asia the plague swept through Europe, leaving millions of dead in its wake. Between a quarter and a third of Europe's population died. In England the population fell from nearly six million to just over three million. The Black Death was the greatest demographic disaster in European history.

The Essential Library

The Crusades by Mike Paine, £3.99

The first crusade was set in motion by Pope Urban II in 1095 and culminated in the capture of Jerusalem from the Muslims four years later. In 1291 the fall of Acre marked the loss of the last Christian enclave in the Holy Land. This Pocket Essential traces the chronology of the Crusades between these two dates and highlights the most important figures on all sides of the conflict.

Alchemy & Alchemists by Sean Martin, £3.99

Alchemy is often seen as an example of medieval gullibility and the alchemists as a collection of eccentrics and superstitious fools. Sean Martin shows that nothing could be further from the truth. It is important to see the search for the philosopher's stone and the attempts to turn base metal into gold as metaphors for the relation of man to nature and man to God as much as seriously held beliefs. Alchemists like Paracelsus and Albertus Magnus were amongst the greatest minds of their time. This book traces the history of alchemy from ancient times to the 20th century, highlighting the interest of modern thinkers like Jung in the subject.

American Civil War by Phil Davies, £3.99

The American Civil War, fought between North and South in the years 1861-1865, was the bloodiest and most traumatic war in American history. Rival visions of the future of the United States faced one another across the battlefields and families and friends were bitterly divided by the conflict. This book examines the deep-rooted causes of the war, so much more complicated than the simple issue of slavery.

American Indian Wars by Howard Hughes, £3.99

At the beginning of the 1840s the proud tribes of the North American Indians looked across the plains at the seemingly unstoppable expansion of the white man's West. During the decades of conflict that followed, as the new world pushed onward, the Indians saw their way of life disappear before their eyes. Over the next 40 years they clung to a dream of freedom and a continuation of their traditions, a dream that was repeatedly shattered by the whites.

The Essential Library: Currently Available

Film Directors:

Woody Allen (Revised)	**Tim Burton**	**Ang Lee**
Jane Campion*	**John Carpenter**	**Steve Soderbergh**
Jackie Chan	**Joel & Ethan Coen**	**Clint Eastwood**
David Cronenberg	**Terry Gilliam***	**Michael Mann**
Alfred Hitchcock	**Krzysztof Kieslowski***	
Stanley Kubrick	**Sergio Leone**	
David Lynch	**Brian De Palma***	
Sam Peckinpah*	**Ridley Scott**	
Orson Welles	**Billy Wilder**	
Steven Spielberg	**Mike Hodges**	

Film Genres:

Blaxploitation Films	**Bollywood**	**French New Wave**
Horror Films	**Slasher Movies**	**Spaghetti Westerns**
Vampire Films*	**Film Noir**	**Heroic Bloodshed***

Film Subjects:

Laurel & Hardy	**Marx Brothers**	**Animation**
Steve McQueen*	**Marilyn Monroe**	**The Oscars®**
Filming On A Microbudget	**Bruce Lee**	**Film Music**

TV:

Doctor Who

Literature:

Cyberpunk	**Philip K Dick**	**The Beat Generation**
Agatha Christie	**Sherlock Holmes**	**Noir Fiction***
Terry Pratchett	**Hitchhiker's Guide**	**Alan Moore**

Ideas:

Conspiracy Theories	**Nietzsche**	**UFOs**
Feminism	**Freud & Psychoanalysis**	

History:

Alchemy & Alchemists	**The Crusades**	**The Black Death**
Jack The Ripper	**The Rise Of New Labour**	**Ancient Greece**
American Civil War	**American Indian Wars**	

Miscellaneous:

The Madchester Scene	**Stock Market Essentials**
How To Succeed As A Sports Agent	

Available at all good bookstores or send a cheque (payable to 'Oldcastle Books') to: **Pocket Essentials (Dept SME), 18 Coleswood Rd, Harpenden, Herts, AL5 1EQ, UK.** £3.99 each (£2.99 if marked with an *) . For each book add 50p postage & packing in the UK and £1 elsewhere.